Strengths

BASED

Parenting

DEVELOPING YOUR CHILDREN'S INNATE TALENTS

FROM GALLUP

MARY RECKMEYER, PH.D.

with JENNIFER ROBISON

GALLUP PRESS
1330 Avenue of the Americas
17th Floor
New York, NY 10019

Library of Congress Control Number: 2014943808
ISBN: 978-1-59562-100-9

First Printing: 2016
10 9 8 7 6 5 4 3 2 1

Printed in Canada

♻ This book was printed on chlorine-free paper made with 100% post-consumer waste.

Donald O. Clifton

1924-2003

Inventor of the Clifton StrengthsFinder® and recognized as the Father of Strengths-Based Psychology by an American Psychological Association Presidential Commendation

Table of Contents

Introduction..1

Chapter One: Setting Kids Up for Success 9

Chapter Two: Can Weaknesses Be Fixed? 19

Chapter Three: There's No "Right" Way to Parent............. 33

Chapter Four: Your Parenting Strengths............................... 43

Chapter Five: Understanding Your Children's Strengths....51

Chapter Six: Strengths-Based Schools.................................. 61

Chapter Seven: Belief, Support, Appreciation 79

The Language of Strengths 87

Clifton StrengthsFinder 93

Clifton Youth StrengthsExplorer 233

StrengthsSpotting 277

References 325

Acknowledgements 337

About the Author..341

"Look at the person sitting to the right of you. And if there's no one on the right, look at the person sitting to the left. That person and you differ at **over a million locations** in your DNA."

— Lee Silver, Ph.D.,
professor of molecular biology and
public policy, Princeton University

Introduction

When you have your first child, you congratulate yourself on how perfect he is or how he sleeps through the night sooner than other babies. Or, you wonder what mistakes you've made because you have a fidgety, fussy baby you wouldn't consider taking to a restaurant or on a long car ride. You either pat yourself on the back or wonder what you're doing wrong.

My first child was that squirmy, high-strung, fussy baby. Around the same time I had him, my best friend had a baby who was calm and always smiling. My friend's baby made parenting look like a piece of cake. I worried about what I needed to do differently, and I was sure I had "ruined" my first born.

And then came baby number two. I had no idea how easy a baby could be. She was naturally even-tempered and content in a car or at a restaurant, and she took long naps. Once I had my second child, I quickly realized that she was her own person. Her adaptability, calm personality and relaxed style were more about who she was than about how I was parenting her. My first child continued to be wiry and active, and during his first two years, he started exhibiting his competitive nature.

After we added two more children to our family, it became more than clear to me that each child enters this world as a unique individual — as most parents will attest. Sure, each one is a composite of his or her parents, but each child is most definitely a unique human being.

And this reality leaves all parents to do the only thing they really can do — parent their children in the way that best enhances each one. But what makes a difference, and how does it matter?

Scientists know more today than ever before about the biological code of DNA, and as research progresses, they will understand it even more clearly. The DNA letters that are the genetic code to each person — A, T, G, C — combine in thousands of ways. The combinations are vast and complex, and the constellations that come together are never exactly the same. That is why we are all unique.

Individuals *are* prewired, but decades of research show that environment also plays a role in development. Studies of identical twins who were raised in different families give insight into the effect of nature and nurture. Who people are and what they become is an inextricably linked outcome of both genetic and environmental influences. Nurture and nature interact to make individuals who they are.

As a parent, you can encourage your children in hundreds of ways, and there are hundreds of things for you to worry and wonder about. Yet even in the midst of your busy and complex daily schedule, you have the opportunity to focus on your children in a way that will have a lasting and positive impact on their lives. You can appreciate their individuality. You can help them see and know their natural affinities — their talents that can become strengths. You can help them explore their interests. And you can build your life — and their lives — on what will help them become productive, happy people.

The miracle of individuality

During my first year of teaching, I was also working to complete a master's degree in educational psychology. It kept me up late at night, but what kept me up even later was trying to unlock the key to each student to help him or her learn. As part of my thesis, I studied students with learning disabilities. That's how I met Steve, a fourth-grade student who quickly validated what I innately knew.

Steve did what he was supposed to do and didn't cause problems in the classroom or at home. His teacher told me that he struggled with math and reading. His mother explained that he had been tested quite a bit and that all of his deficits had been identified. When I interviewed Steve, he confirmed everything I already knew from his teacher and his mom. Steve's identity and activities were wrapped up in what were considered his inadequacies.

For my study, the assessment I used was a one-on-one interview with open-ended questions designed to identify strengths and interests. When I would ask parents and other teachers for permission to interview children, most were excited and happy to help. But Steve's mom said, "Well, we already know what's wrong with him, and we have had lots of tests." His teacher also responded by saying she already knew what was wrong and was working on it — he had issues with math, reading and social skills. And it was clear that connecting with Steve was challenging.

My first interview with Steve was painful — for me. I asked him questions, and after lengthy and awkward pauses, he responded with short answers. Toward the end of the interview, I said to him, "Tell me what you like to do in your free time." He responded that he didn't have friends to hang out with and that he mostly just watched TV.

And then just before I moved to the next question, something sparked him to add, "There's this one show I like where the guy shows you how to draw. I watch it and draw whenever it's on." I had promised Steve's mom and teacher some feedback, but he didn't give me much to work with. Grasping at straws, as we concluded, I told Steve that I'd love to see his drawings sometime.

Monday morning rolled around, and as I sat at my desk getting ready for classes to start, I heard some shuffling. I looked up and saw Steve. He simply dropped some papers on my desk. The papers had his sketches on them. And each day, he returned with more drawings. We quickly became friends. That someone simply cared, listened, accepted and appreciated something he could do — not all the problems that overwhelmed him — was powerful. It changed Steve. By the time he was in fifth grade, he had become a kid who liked school, who improved in math and reading, and who made three new friends.

This doesn't sound like a miraculous story, and yet it is. Steve isn't some wonder kid who went on to become famous, but he is a kid who grew from who he *was* instead of who he wasn't. And in that sense, he is the miracle that each of us should be.

This story could be true for thousands of kids — kids who should be defined by what they *can* do and who they *can* become versus who they aren't. For Steve, that meant someone appreciating who he was beyond math, reading and relating.

As a result, the significant adults in Steve's life saw him through a new lens. They started to display Steve's art. He drew a lot of cartoons and had a sense of humor that other kids could relate to. When you're at that age, drawing and cartooning are revered talents. They gave Steve a new identity. Instead of being the kid who couldn't read or write well or who didn't know math, he became known as the funny kid who could draw.

And isn't that what we want for all people — to be known for what they can do instead of what they can't do? It does take a village to raise a child. And it does take diversity, acceptance and many different talents to make the world not only turn, but be productive. Our future doesn't depend on everybody being the same; it depends on each person sharing his talents, his blessings, his beliefs and his passions.

An immense amount of research on human development has brought to light that you do your best when you're doing what you're best at — when you're using your strengths — and that goes for your children too. Every parent and every child is unique. There is no one right way to bring up a child. There is only the way you do it, given your talents, strengths and environment.

But there *are* ways to do what you do better with less stress and more happiness. You can develop as a parent and help your children develop as individuals too.

I have spent decades studying individuals and what makes them tick. From mentoring to teaching to researching to collaborating with hundreds of educators — as well as raising a family — I have become convinced that what makes the biggest developmental difference in someone's life is having at least one person who not only loves and cares about him but who also recognizes and respects his individuality. Someone who encourages him to excel. Someone who sees the best in him. Someone who helps him find pathways that take him in positive directions. I want to help you be that someone for your children. I want to help you understand and develop your own strengths and your children's potential.

The goal of this book is to change the way the world views parenting. Powered by the profound science and simple tools of Gallup's strengths-based development research in workplaces, schools and countries worldwide, *Strengths Based Parenting* will show you key insights from Gallup's research into the ingredients of a life well-lived and parenting approaches that build on parents' and children's talents. As you read the stories and practical advice on how to develop talents and strengths, manage weaknesses, and partner with schools and teachers, you are taking the first step on your family's strengths journey and making a difference in their future.

"I wondered if there was a

lost generation of people

who succumbed because their

**fuel tanks were a little

smaller** than mine."

———————————————————

— Neil deGrasse Tyson, Ph.D.,
astrophysicist

CHAPTER ONE

Setting Kids Up for Success

From the day you discover a baby is on the way, questions start mounting. And they continue as the little one grows up: How do you get a child to sleep through the night? Is it OK for your child to sleep in your bed? When is the best time to potty train? Should both parents work outside the home? Will your child turn out better or worse if she's allowed to jump on the furniture in your home? How much screen time is OK? Can your child play sports *and* be a musician? What time should his curfew be? Which college is the right one?

There isn't a "right" answer to any of these questions because the right answer for most questions depends on you, your child and your family. But to put these kinds of issues in perspective, they are less important for a child's later success in life than you might think.

By success, I don't mean wealth or status. By success, I mean happiness, fulfillment and a life well-lived — a life with everything your child needs and most of what he wants. And, crucially, a life in which he has the ability to use his talents to create an environment that sustains and motivates him with the people he cares about and who care about him. That's success. Fortunately, those elements of success *are* things parents can directly influence.

There is a great deal of emotional pressure on parents to do a good job and a lot of anxiety triggered by books and articles that highlight the damage done by poor parenting or lost opportunities by not parenting enough. It takes a long time to see the difference that all your investment makes. The day-to-day business of parenting is full of ups and downs, frustrations and joy, and hard work — without mechanisms in place to evaluate whether you are doing a good job. Parenting requires more responsibility and has more impact on the future than most people's professional work, yet there is no formal or prescribed training.

While there isn't a "prescription for parenting," studying the childhood of adults who are doing well reveals common threads, common experiences and a common belief among their parents. Decades of studies — from Victor and Mildred George Goertzel's *Cradles of Eminence* to Benjamin Bloom's *Developing Talent in Young People* to Mihaly Csikszentmihalyi and Barbara Schneider's *Becoming Adult* — suggest that those commonalities are: Treat children as individuals. Respect their natural inclinations, talents and interests.

Stoking fuel tanks

When Jason Wu was a child growing up in Taiwan, his parents didn't know how he would make a living, but they did see his passion. Today, while he may be best known for creating Michelle Obama's inaugural gowns, Wu has become a leader in the worlds of fashion design and retail. What made a difference in his childhood? Wu credits his parents.

When Wu was a boy, his teacher told his mother that Wu needed to quit playing so much and to start concentrating on his studies. But, according to Abel Cheng, founder of parenting blog

Parent Wonder, "His mother knew the importance of discovering a child's talent and [letting] it shine. His mother knew doing what the majority was doing was not going to help [her] son. His mother knew to be happy and successful, one had to follow his passion — no matter how silly it may look."

While his brother spent a lot of time playing with video games and robots, Jason preferred dolls. His parents didn't discourage him. In fact, they bought him dolls. When he was 9, he begged his mother for a sewing machine. He got one for Christmas and spent a great deal of time creating doll outfits. And his mother would drive him to bridal stores so he could sketch the gowns in the windows.

"I think having parents who understood [me] was a blessing," Wu said. "Because otherwise, I probably would have just become a misunderstood child."

"The Master of the Universe" and perhaps America's best known astrophysicist, Neil deGrasse Tyson, says his world expanded after a visit to the Hayden Planetarium when he too was 9. From that day forward, he knew he wanted to learn as much as possible about the universe. Having the support of his parents fueled his passion. They gave him a telescope after that first visit. And they encouraged and allowed him to develop his expertise.

This expertise gave Tyson a strong sense of self and confidence to persevere, which a black kid from the Bronx in the 1960s needed if he wanted to be an astrophysicist. "I was an aspiring astrophysicist and that's how I defined myself, not by my skin color," he told *Parade* magazine. "I was just glad I had something to think about other than how society was treating me. Teachers would say, 'You should join this or that team,' not the physics club. My fuel tank had been stoked since I was 9, but it took some energy to overcome the resistance. I wondered if there was a lost generation of people who succumbed because their fuel tanks were a little smaller than mine."

"Stoking fuel tanks" is something all parents can do — noticing a child's interests, giving her time to explore and learn about those interests, and helping her become good at something. Her interests may be dinosaurs, numbers, drawing, experimenting or building with blocks. Being able to pursue an interest and become an expert in it takes your child to another level, or even another area, and it encourages her to continue the quest of learning and finding her niche. That may be as a great designer, astrophysicist, teacher, rancher, salesperson or humanitarian.

Helping your child discover that niche and create a successful life is much easier when you know and use your talents and strengths and help your child use hers. People are most effective when they're working from their strengths. And doing what you do best makes you happier too.

Strengths theory

Gallup has been studying strengths for decades. These studies are rooted in the early work of my father, Dr. Don Clifton. He was an educational psychology professor who studied what was right with people and what contributed to their success at a time when the field of psychology was focused on researching deficits and what was wrong with people. The American Psychological Association named Clifton the Father of Strengths-Based Psychology, and his work launched a whole new area of research for the thousands of scientists who followed him.

In the 1990s, under Clifton's leadership, Gallup developed the Clifton StrengthsFinder assessment as an objective measure of personal talent that could be administered online in less than one hour. The instrument identifies 34 themes of talent — areas where an individual's greatest potential for building strengths exists. The Clifton StrengthsFinder report provides people with a list of their top five themes of talent. As of this writing, more than 12 million people have taken the Clifton StrengthsFinder assessment in more than 25 languages. *See the Clifton StrengthsFinder section of the book for definitions and more about each of the 34 talent themes.*

34 Clifton StrengthsFinder Themes

Achiever	Connectedness	Harmony	Relator
Activator	Consistency	Ideation	Responsibility
Adaptability	Context	Includer	Restorative
Analytical	Deliberative	Individualization	Self-Assurance
Arranger	Developer	Input	Significance
Belief	Discipline	Intellection	Strategic
Command	Empathy	Learner	Woo
Communication	Focus	Maximizer	
Competition	Futuristic	Positivity	

To clarify the distinction between talents and strengths, Gallup has specific definitions for both: A *talent* is a natural way of thinking, feeling or behaving. A *strength* is the result of taking that talent and, with investment — skills, knowledge and practice — using it to consistently provide near-perfect performance in a given activity — for example, analyzing information, visualizing future possibilities or recognizing the unique qualities of each person.

Talent (a natural way of thinking, feeling or behaving)

Investment (time spent practicing, developing your skills and building your knowledge base)

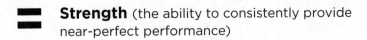

Strength (the ability to consistently provide near-perfect performance)

People are not always aware of their talents though. Talents are so innate, so ever-present, that you might not even realize you have them. In fact, people typically think that whatever talents they have, everybody has. That's how closely entwined your talents are with your behaviors and your perception of the world.

"I was in 4-H as a kid just like everyone else I knew, except I was in *all* the 4-H clubs," says Matt, who grew up on a farm in Iowa. "Most people did a couple of livestock clubs, girls did a sewing or cooking club too, and boys would do a science thing. But over the years, I took every single club that would let me in. And I did really, really well — I almost always purpled at the State Fair [purple ribbons are awarded to outstanding projects]. But here's the thing. When I purpled, I quit the club. When I'm done, I'm done."

Many of the grown-ups around Matt told him he needed to quit jumping from activity to activity. "I was always hearing that I was a quitter, I lacked follow-through, blah, blah, blah. And really, things haven't changed. I'll get totally into something, find success, and then, I'm done." When Matt and his dad sat down to review his top five Clifton StrengthsFinder themes — Achiever, Activator, Maximizer,

Input and Competition — his dad realized that Matt loves to learn and that he feels like he *has* to get started, work hard and win.

Matt's father pointed out to him that he does well because he works extremely hard. But once he learns what he wants to know and does what he wants to do, he's ready to do the next thing. It was Matt's ability to initiate and make things happen that set him apart. Other people can maintain their interest, but once Matt wins, he's done. With his father's support, Matt continued to find new projects he could initiate and complete successfully before moving on to the next challenge.

Would it surprise you to learn that Matt is a serial entrepreneur? He has started several businesses — the first from his dorm room when he was a freshman in college. And he sold all of them as soon as he got them off the ground. Matt likes to learn and build, but he doesn't like to run things. "For years, I felt kind of bad, like people were right that I have a character flaw," he says. "But my dad helped me see that I'm a great builder, not a great manager. And the world needs builders."

That's what's so exciting about taking the Clifton StrengthsFinder assessment. It shows you that the things that have always come so easily to you — building and learning, for example — are actually pretty special. What comes easily to you is where you have talents. The most important thing to remember about your talents is that they are your areas of greatest potential and where you have an innate capacity for excellence.

That innate capacity for excellence is one of the first aspects of talent my dad noticed when he began studying it. Early on, he conducted a study of reading speed among students. Some of the students were fast readers, and others were slower. All of the kids took part in a course to increase their reading speed and comprehension, and all of them improved. But the fast readers improved more than the slow readers did. In fact, the fast readers more than tripled their reading speed. The speediest readers grew the most and benefited the most from more training.

Strengths and self-perception

Research suggests that self-perception is related to various aspects of academic achievement, social status, participation, school completion and perception of others. And a parent's perception of a child and the child's perception of himself have an impact not only on the parent-child relationship, but also on the child's growth and later success. Self-perception and confidence are largely influenced by previous achievement. A child takes his first step, his parents clap and he thinks, "I'll try another step."

Merely telling a child he can succeed is not enough. To believe he can succeed, he has to actually experience success. Self-concept of ability influences achievement, and achievement influences self-concept of ability. Understanding this interaction is essential. That's why efforts to increase self-esteem don't work if they're not authentic. Think back — did your "participant" awards increase your motivation in team activities? Or did a first-place medal make you want to stay involved?

So what does this have to do with talents and strengths? To help your children succeed and develop confidence and a healthy self-perception, you need to identify the areas where they have the most capacity for success — in other words, their talents. You also need to create a positive, supportive environment where your children can apply those talents and build them into strengths.

Many studies have indicated that environment affects a child's intellect, skill development and socialization. An environment that is full of positive experiences and emotions and that supports your child's talents will not only promote his self-perception, it will lay the foundation for other meaningful life outcomes. Barbara Fredrickson, the Kenan distinguished professor of psychology and principal investigator of the Positive Emotions and Psychophysiology Laboratory at the University of North Carolina at Chapel Hill, notes that "positive emotions are not trivial luxuries, but instead are critical necessities for optimal functioning." Her research shows that positive emotions:

- protect people from, and can undo the effects of, negative emotions

- fuel resilience and transform people

- broaden thinking, encouraging people to discover new lines of thought or action

- break down racial barriers

- build durable physical, intellectual, social and psychological resources that can function as "reserves" during trying times

- produce optimal functioning in organizations and individuals

Remember, as a parent, you have a direct influence on your children's lives from the day they are born. Each day, we experience about 20,000 individual moments, according to Nobel Prize-winning scientist Daniel Kahneman, but we really remember only the positive and negative ones. You have the power to make more of those 20,000 moments positive and memorable for your children every day. You can create the environment that is right for *your* children and *your* family and set them up for success — happiness, fulfillment and a life well-lived.

"Don't let what you **cannot do** interfere with what you **can do.**"

— John Wooden (1910-2010),
American basketball player and coach

CHAPTER TWO

Can Weaknesses Be Fixed?

"[There is] the belief that strengths are the opposite of weaknesses, illness is the opposite of health, success is the opposite of failure, good is the opposite of bad. They are not. ... Yet we are tricked into believing that if we find out what went wrong and fix it, everything will be right; if we identify our weaknesses, we can turn them into strengths. In fact, however, we cannot learn about strengths by studying and focusing on weaknesses. Studying broken homes will not lead to information on building strong families. Studying why young people use drugs will not lead us to an understanding of the conditions under which some children say no to drugs. Studying why kids fail at math will not explain why some students excel."

This quote is from the book *Soar With Your Strengths*, coauthored by my father, Don Clifton. As the quote suggests — in sharp contrast to conventional wisdom — strengths are not the opposite of weaknesses, and you can't turn your weaknesses into strengths. Still, many people spend their lives trying to overcome and "fix" their weaknesses. But no matter how hard you work, the best you may achieve in an area of weakness is mediocrity. You'll accomplish a lot more by improving on a talent than by trying to fix a weakness.

So ask yourself, on an average day, how much time do your children devote to honing their talents? And how much time do they spend deep in the weeds of their weaknesses, trying to work on or fix them?

Take Susan, for example. Her top five themes include Command, Self-Assurance and Maximizer, which can all be useful for business leaders. And, in fact, Susan owns a successful real estate company. "I use my themes every day, and I think they've helped make me be successful professionally," she says. "But I didn't think so when I was a kid when everybody was calling me bossy, pushy and demanding." Susan grew up in the 1960s and thinks that if she'd been a boy, people would have felt different about her. "They'd have said I had leadership potential. Instead, I was told I'd never catch a husband unless I changed my attitude."

Susan believed what she was told. After all, she wanted a happy life. But the future that adults were spelling out for her didn't paint that picture. She found relief in sports, where girls were allowed to be "bossy, pushy and demanding." But otherwise, she forced herself to be quiet, hang back and let others lead.

"Even when it was obvious that things were on the wrong track, I just bit my tongue," she says. "And I thought I was doing the right thing. I had friends, I married a great guy, I had a happy family — all the things I was told I wouldn't have if I didn't tone myself down."

Things finally changed when Susan opened her own company, which allowed her to be bossy, pushy and demanding — and get rewarded for it. "It makes me think that no matter how hard you stomp your strengths down and concentrate on your weaknesses, your strengths will pop back up," she says. "My strengths are perfect for running a company like mine. But boy, I wish I'd known that 30 years ago. I wasted *decades* being pretty good at selling real estate, when I could have been doing something I love — running a real estate company."

Susan's experience isn't all that unusual. Even today, parents and teachers are more likely to focus on what's wrong with a child rather than on what's right. In fact, a Gallup survey showed that 52% of Americans believe that knowing what your weaknesses are and attempting to improve them will help you be more successful in your life than knowing what your strengths are and attempting to build on them. And 77% of U.S. parents say the subjects in which a child gets the worst grades deserve the most time and attention. There's a name for this way of thinking: the deficit-based development model.

People using this model to raise or teach children search out the shortcomings in a child's cognitive, social and educational development. Once those deficits are detected, fixing them becomes a priority.

The problem is, deficit-based development models don't work that well. In fact, a 2004 study of deficit-based programs aimed at keeping at-risk kids out of jail found that the programs were likely to have a harmful effect and actually increased the kids' delinquency, relative to doing nothing at all. That's not really surprising. Many years ago, I spent time at a state correctional facility for young men aged 18-24. My interviews with them revealed that they were readily aware of their shortcomings and equally unaware of any personal assets. They knew what they shouldn't do, but they didn't know what they could do, what paths to take and what resources to rely on when they took a wrong turn.

If a child only knows what she is not good at, she doesn't know how to create pathways that give her direction. She needs to be able to manage her weaknesses so they don't become stumbling blocks, and she also needs stepping stones to move forward.

Nonetheless, a lot of people were raised to believe that they needed to fix their weaknesses but their talents could take care of themselves. So, like Susan, they gave less time to their talents, and their weaknesses took center stage. They put a lot of time and energy into things that they didn't like and didn't become very good at, hoping they could change. But they really can't.

Just as talents are innate, so are weaknesses. There are things you're naturally great at and things you're not. You can try to improve in an area of weakness, and you can get better. But being mediocre may be as good as you'll get. And wasting so much time and energy becoming adequate means *not* putting time and effort into an area of talent, where you could become extraordinary. There's a much better way to deal with weaknesses: manage them.

Managing weaknesses

Roy Spence says he experienced an epiphany when he was 14. "I was in eighth grade and we had to do a class essay on Ralph Waldo Emerson, whom I love. I turned in the essay, and when I got it back I had nine misspelled words with big red circles everywhere and a big C on the right side of the paper. C's were not celebrated in the Spence home, but my mom said nothing. I thought, 'Wow — got away with that one.'

"The next year in ninth grade we were studying Emerson again. And when test time came around, I said, 'Mom, I can't do this paper! I will get another C!' She said, 'Roy, just do the best you can.' So I turned in the paper, and when I got it back the whole paper was covered with red circles around misspelled words. I looked up, and on the top-right side of the page was a very small A-.

"I ran home and held the two papers in front of my mom. 'Mom, I don't get it.' She paused and stared at the two papers — each covered with a sea of red circles — and looked me straight in the eye. 'Son, you can't spell.' Long pause. 'But you can write. So here is the grand bargain I am going to make with you at 14 years of age. I want you to try hard, study hard and do the very best you can at everything in school. But in life, I do not want you to waste any of your precious time or talent trying to be average at what you are bad at. I want you to spend your life becoming great at what you are good at … play to your strengths in life, serving others and the greater good, and you will be happy and fulfilled — and the world will be just a little bit better.'

"So, I am passing on the wisdom of my mother. Play to your strengths. Serve others and the greater good, and you won't have to spend a lot of your life searching for meaning and happiness; meaning and happiness will meet you where you are."

That was liberating to Spence, who went on to co-found a national marketing communications and advertising company as well as author several books. He says, "Without mom, I would have thought I was a failure because I couldn't spell."

The way to manage weaknesses is this: Do what you need to do so that weaknesses don't get in the way of your goals. If your child shows a serious weakness in some area, don't force her to focus on it in hopes that she'll triumph over it. She won't. If she has horrible handwriting, have her practice until it is legible and let it go at that. If she struggles with reading, find ways to help her, but be sure she gets to read things that interest her. If she's disorganized, help set her up with an easy-to-use system. Let her keep her papers in one big folder, not an elaborate organizational system.

Anthony's 9-year-old daughter is constantly losing things. He explains, "She lost her winter coat in February. The school library has revoked her privileges to check out books every year since first grade because she loses books *before she leaves the library*. Last weekend, she went to a swimming party and came home with one shoe. Who doesn't notice they're only wearing one shoe?"

That was the last straw for Anthony. As he searched the neighborhood for one shoe, he realized that this situation wasn't going to get better. He could remind his daughter about her belongings every time she left home for the rest of her life, but she'd still lose them. "Not being able to keep track of things is an innate characteristic of hers, and I can't change it. So I gave up trying," Anthony says. "However, being a creature of habit is also an innate characteristic of hers, and that's what I decided to concentrate on."

Anthony knows that once his daughter develops a routine, it sticks. "Unlike our other kids, we never have to remind her to brush her teeth or feed the dog. She does it automatically because it's part of her routine," he says. So Anthony made keeping track of objects, some of them anyway, part of his daughter's routine. And he did it with a roll of masking tape.

"I let her decide the best place for her coat, shoes and backpack, and then I made a square around those spots with masking tape. Now we have a tape square on the kitchen floor, a tape square in the car and a tape square in my in-laws' mudroom, because she visits Grandma and Grandpa after school a lot. She comes in, she sees the square, and it reminds her to put her things there and not wherever they happen to fall out of her hands."

There's nothing special about these tape squares. They're not magic spaces that will keep a kid from losing things. But Anthony thinks that because his daughter has a talent for routine, putting things she'd otherwise misplace in those taped-off squares — and only in those squares — will become a habit. "I remind her about the squares every day, but she doesn't really need me to. And we talk about how she'll just have to make imaginary squares whenever she's in a new place, and

I hope it works," Anthony says. "But I also know that she'll lose stuff. It's just the way she is."

Your areas of weakness are where you find the most obstacles and stress. Anthony's daughter is lucky because she has a talent for being routine-oriented that she can use to combat her weakness. But not every weakness has an opposing talent. Being good at making friends doesn't make up for having a weakness in math, for example. Still, being good at making friends is a talent that a child can capitalize on. And capitalizing on talents can go a long way toward a happier, healthier life, as Gallup research shows.

Millions of Clifton StrengthsFinder assessments, thousands of interviews and research into well-being reveal that focusing on your talents and strengths has a positive influence on your quality of life. According to Gallup's studies:

- The more Americans use their strengths to do what they do best, the less likely they are to report experiencing physical pain, worry, stress, anger or sadness the prior day, even when they have health problems.

- The more Americans use their strengths to do what they do best, the more likely they are to report a boost in positive emotions such as enjoyment and happiness and to report having ample energy, feeling well-rested, being happy, smiling or laughing a lot, learning something interesting, and being treated with respect.

- People who have the opportunity to focus on their strengths every day are more than three times as likely to report having an excellent quality of life and are six times as likely to be engaged in their jobs.

- A strengths-based approach can improve your confidence, direction, hope and kindness toward others.

Your children's future selves

Leah Adler raised her son and three daughters in Scottsdale, Arizona. Her kids are adults now and have created successful lives for themselves. But Leah had reason to worry about one of her kids, Steve, who struggled more in school than his sisters did. Steve had dyslexia that went undiagnosed for years, so he wasn't a great student. His parents divorced when he was in high school, which caused him difficulties. And he had trouble completing tasks — at least those he didn't enjoy. When the neighbors hired him to paint, he quit before the job was done. His mom finished the painting for him.

Some might think Leah should have pushed Steve to stay on task, to work harder in school and to correct his weaknesses. Instead, Leah supported Steve's talents and interests. When he was 11 and wanted to earn a Boy Scout badge in photography, she packed a lunch and drove all the kids out to the desert so Steve could make a movie. By the time he was 14, Steve was so interested in making home movies that he talked Leah into buying 30 cans of cherries — and then exploding them out of a pressure cooker while he filmed the whole thing.

Meanwhile, Steve's grades weren't getting better, classmates were bullying him and the neighbors probably weren't hiring him to paint. If Leah had parented by the deficit model, she'd have doubled down on fixing his weaknesses. But she didn't. She cleaned up the exploded cherries and let Steve focus on making movies, the thing he loved and had a genuine interest in.

And focusing on making home movies put Steve in a position to cope with his weaknesses. "I never felt like a victim," Steve said later about his undiagnosed dyslexia. "Movies really helped me … kind of saved me from shame, from guilt. Making movies was my great escape. When I felt like an outsider, movies made me feel inside my own skill set."

People who know, develop and use their talents, as Steve did, have a direction, a mechanism for productivity. When a child is allowed to expand in his areas of interest and talent, it's easier for him to find success and harder for him to define himself by his weaknesses.

It doesn't really matter what a child's talents and interests are, but letting him have in-depth exploration does. Following an interest may lead to specific expertise or it may lead to something else entirely, but your child finding his own path is crucial. To develop a healthy sense of pride, confidence and identity, your child has to know what his talents are — and be able to develop them into strengths.

Leah let Steve explore his talents and his interests, and he eventually used them to develop a career behind the camera. He got pretty good at it. You may have even seen some of his work, which includes *Jaws*, *E.T.*, the *Indiana Jones* movies, *Schindler's List* and dozens of other films he has directed or produced under his full name: Steven Spielberg.

Leah Adler gave her children the opportunity to value and explore their interests and talents. Not every kid gets that chance. And, of course, not every kid who likes making movies is going to grow up to be Steven Spielberg. But encouraging a child to do more of what he does best can make a difference now and years down the road. You don't know who your kids are going to become, but you can help them develop their future selves.

Human beings are complex, and understanding how to bring out the best in others is an ongoing process. It's hard to know exactly where to steer yourself or your child. Leah Adler didn't actually know where Steve was going with the home movies, just that he really enjoyed making them. She says about her son, "When he was growing up, I didn't know he was a genius. Frankly, I didn't know what the hell he was. I'm really ashamed, but I didn't recognize the symptoms of talent. I had no idea back then that my son would be Steven Spielberg."

Paying attention to talent

In *Developing Talent in Young People*, Dr. Benjamin Bloom — the preeminent education theorist behind Bloom's Taxonomy — says the exceptionally talented very often received public recognition for their talent in elementary school. While some outstanding young people and adults regularly receive public recognition — for example, athletes, musicians, math geniuses and artists — most do not. What if we recognized *everyone's* unique talents, whether those talents were for organizing, volunteering, taking responsibility, being funny or being punctual? How much would a child's talent develop if she got recognition for it?

Yet it's so easy to focus on kids' weaknesses. And too often, parents and schools push children to be well-rounded and "good" at everything. But the goal is to nurture kids so they can find what makes them happiest and most successful and so they can build their lives around that. The best thing you can do is challenge your children in a way that inspires them to work toward growth and success.

I know a successful executive of a global company who struggled in school. As an adult, she was diagnosed with attention deficit hyperactivity disorder (ADHD), which didn't surprise her because she had such a horrible time, especially in college. She wasn't able to concentrate and flunked or barely passed a lot of easy courses. "Those classes were disorienting — I just had no idea what the professor or the students were talking about," she says. But her father noticed what she was good at, and he pointed her in the direction of sales. When he did, he gave her some simple, yet profound, wisdom. He told her that her weaknesses would never develop, but that her strengths would develop infinitely.

Following her father's advice, she got a job selling records, and then a better job selling tapes, and then an even better job selling ads. She was thriving at sales. She says, "It was perfect, because the two things that inspired me most in a job were salesmanship and ideas. I still love ideas, even bad ones." Her top five themes are Futuristic, Ideation, Competition, Activator and Woo. For her, selling was a dream come true. Eventually, she and a friend borrowed $5,000 to launch a company — and that company is now global, wealthy and influential. "None of this would have happened without my dad's advice. It was the best advice I ever received. If he hadn't taught me this, my development and achievements would have stopped at a very early age — in college, probably," she says.

As a parent, you have a huge influence on the way your kids learn to manage what doesn't come naturally to them. But you need to recognize and manage your own weaknesses too. If staying on task is a weak spot for you, don't spend weekends creating systems that force you to finish what you start. Play with the kids instead. Your kids are going to benefit from the time you spend with them much more than those systems ever will. And how long are you going to pay attention to systems that chain you to a weakness anyway?

As you manage your own weaknesses and help your children manage theirs, keep these things in mind:

- Explore your talents, and work on developing them into strengths. Integrate them into your daily life.

- Spend as little time and energy in your areas of weakness as you can. Stop trying to fix yourself. You don't need to become well-rounded. You are better off spending your time and energy in your areas of talent.

- Explore your children's talents with them. Show them that they are capable of greatness. Help them turn their natural talents into strengths. Tell them there will be obstacles that get in their way, and help them remove those obstacles.

- Recognize that while your children's peers and culture are influential, parents and grandparents can give children a strong foundation of hope and resilience for the future.

There will always be things you need to do that you don't necessarily enjoy or aren't particularly good at. To graduate from high school, you have to pass English, even if you hate reading. To get an expense reimbursement, you have to turn in an expense report, even if you hate sorting out receipts. Don't ignore your weaknesses, but understand that you will be better able to cope with them when you know your talents and strengths and when you have experienced success. The key is managing your weaknesses so they don't become obstacles to excellence.

The same is true for children. As adults, we need to be careful about how we judge kids. We can make them doubt themselves. We can make it harder for them to be great. We can even crush them. But we can't really change them. We can't make them who they aren't, but we can make it easier and happier for them to be who they are.

"We must look on children in need **not as problems but as individuals with potential** ... I would hope we could find creative ways to draw out of our children **the good that there is in each of them.**"

— Archbishop Desmond Tutu,
1984 Nobel Peace Prize laureate

CHAPTER THREE

There's No "Right" Way to Parent

Parenting and child-rearing theories have been around for a long time. From the Torah to Twitter, there's always been advice on how to bring up children.

Some ideas have turned out to be more detrimental than others. For instance, in a 1928 parenting book, behavioral psychologist John B. Watson wrote that parents should "never hug or kiss children." Rather, parents should demonstrate affection by shaking hands with their children every morning. Apparently, Watson thought hugging kids would give them unreasonable expectations for the future.

Thankfully, that recommendation is no longer taken seriously. On the other hand, now there's new advice that can be confusing: Let kids have lots of social interaction, but not too much. Children need to sleep just the right amount of time. Give kids vitamins, but not too many. Make sure they get lots of time outside, but beware of sun exposure. Encourage kids to express themselves in the arts, athletics and academics — but no pressure to win. OK, some pressure. The right kind.

Clearly, there's no one way to parent. And parents have always wondered if they were doing it right. More than 200 years ago, Abigail

Adams used to discuss child development theories with her friends and family. And her preferred parenting theorist, Reverend James Fordyce, sounded surprisingly modern, telling parents to understand and support personal growth and individual development in their children. Still, there are many people who would like you to adopt their ideas about child rearing.

The reason there is so much debate and so much advice about the proper way to parent is because children are our future. But, there isn't a magic pill or a one-size-fits-all way to raise *your* child.

Everyone has talents

Dr. Temple Grandin was born in 1947. Her parents were told she had autism when she was 2 years old. She didn't speak until she was 4. By the time she was a teenager, other kids called her "tape recorder" because of her habit of repeating things. Fortunately for Temple, her parents chose to concentrate on what she was capable of. And she turned out to be capable of a lot: three degrees, an incredible career in education, a leading advocate for animal welfare, and a beacon of hope and compassion in the autism community. But if Franklin Pierce University, where she earned her bachelor's degree, had required algebra for her to graduate, she likely would not have become the Temple Grandin the world now knows. She said, "I can't do algebra. It makes no sense. Why does algebra have to be the gateway to all the other mathematics?"

Parents might not realize just how much they expect of their children until they have one who doesn't meet the usual expectations. As T. Berry Brazelton and Stanley I. Greenspan say in their seminal book, *The Irreducible Needs of Children: What Every Child Must Have to Grow, Learn, and Flourish*, "Parents have long known and accepted that each of their children is different. We can now provide tools to confirm this intuitive impression, but more important, to systematize it so that parents can use their insights to promote healthy development in each of their children, not just the ones who fit more easily into the expectable family patterns."

Every family develops its own patterns according to its own values, but society also has patterns it expects a child to fit into. Parents watch for the age their child speaks his first word, the distance he can run in a minute, whether or not he knows the solar system, how he does on his SAT — or if he can even take the test, and they compare those numbers to every other kid's results. They look to the expectable patterns to see how their child fits, or doesn't.

I'm not saying those patterns aren't important. But they're not important in the same way for every child. Some kids are not going to know the planets of the solar system. Some kids are going to know the solar system so well that the solar system is all they want to talk about. Both kinds of kids have something to offer the world and themselves.

Remember Anthony, the dad who used tape squares so his daughter wouldn't lose her shoes and book bag every day? Anthony's wife, Camil, says, "The school psychologist thinks it might be attention deficit disorder or autism. So what are you supposed to do with a kid like that? How are you supposed to help if you don't know what's wrong? I'm scared to death that a kid who can't keep track of her shoes is going to be an adult who can't hold down a job."

Is Camil worrying too much? It's easy to dismiss her fears about her child — lots of perfectly successful people started out as the kind of children who lose shoes — when that child isn't yours. But when the child *is* yours and *isn't* meeting typical expectations, fear is a rational reaction, especially in a world that has so many expectations.

Heather and Scott understand. They started out parenthood with triplets and then added a fourth child, Nick, to their family. Nick has Down syndrome. For Heather and Scott, that meant facing a lot of unknowns. "When you have a special needs kid, you are constantly bombarded by people who point out what he can't do," they explain. "He can't keep up with a typically developing classroom. He can't perform. There are so many 'cant's' that others are quick to point out. And there are so many times we are told and can see the things Nick can't do. That doesn't help us with his future.

"But noticing Nick's strengths does give us another focus. He struggles with sequencing numbers but flourishes with double-digit math and addition. Or when we see how he relates to people, we see the things he can do in the future, and in turn, we can help him see what he can do." Noticing Nick's abilities helps his family, teachers and coaches go beyond remediation. Focusing on what Nick *can* do gives them ways to motivate, develop and support him.

Everyone needs some backup help. Sometimes that means taping squares on the floor. Sometimes it means lifelong professional medical, developmental or psychological assistance. But every child needs help learning to use his or her talents because while all children have challenges, they also all have gifts. They all have talents. And parents need to help, support and encourage children to recognize those talents and applaud them as they develop their talents into strengths. And every child *can* do that, in his or her own way.

Jeff wasn't "supposed" to be an artist

When Julie and Hal Hanson's son Jeff was 12, doctors found a tumor on his optic nerve. Jeff underwent weeks of chemotherapy and radiation. Friends and family would come to visit him as he recuperated, but it was awkward. As Julie says, "What do you say to a kid who's hairless?" To make it easier on everyone, Julie and Hal put out some notecards and art supplies so that Jeff and his visitors would have something to do together. Julie kept the notecards she especially liked and tossed out the rest. After a while, she noticed that the ones she was keeping were Jeff's. "Until then, I had no clue he had artistic talent," she says.

A few months later when he was feeling better, Jeff asked if he could set up a lemonade stand at the end of the driveway to make some spending money. But instead of lemonade, he would sell his notecards and Julie's baked goods. People loved Jeff's notecards. They loved them a *lot*: Jeff wound up selling $15,000 worth of his art. "Jeff wasn't supposed to be an artist," Hal said later in an interview. "This is so surreal that I just don't even know how to interpret it."

Hal, Julie and Jeff decided to divide the proceeds: one-third for Jeff to spend, one-third for Jeff to save and one-third for charity. They encouraged Jeff to develop this newfound talent. Hal and Julie built a workshop for him in their unfinished basement and stocked it with paper and canvases, new paints, and colors. Soon Jeff was selling paintings. And then more of them. And then lots more. By the age of 19, Jeff Hanson had sold roughly 1,300 works of art and donated $1 million to various charities. That sounds easier than it was. Jeff had some difficulties on his path, and his parents worked to help him overcome them.

One challenge is that Jeff has ADD, and he struggled at school. Julie knew that Jeff had a natural need for structure, so she and Jeff made a chart with his everyday routine and the things he needed to accomplish, and they hung it on the refrigerator. Jeff's love of lists and being able to check off his accomplishments gave his world structure and incentive.

That helped with the ADD struggles, but there's nothing Julie and Hal could do to help Jeff overcome another challenge: He is legally blind. The tumor on his optic nerve and subsequent treatment destroyed Jeff's eyesight when he was 12. Every work of art Jeff has made since then — the pictures he made during chemo and radiation treatment; the notecards he sold at the end of the driveway; the paintings that sell for tens of thousands of dollars; and lately, couture dresses and even a Porsche — they were all created by a kid who can barely see.

Julie and Hal realized that Jeff had a natural talent, and they did everything they could to help him make the most of it. They also recognized that he had serious weaknesses, and they helped him work around them. Jeff has become hugely successful because he and his family decided early on that he should direct his energies toward his talents and strengths.

Giving children what they need most

Children learn and grow better when they put their energy toward what they *can* do rather than slaving away on what they struggle with. So do parents. Kids thrive when parents recognize what they do well and give themselves some slack for not being perfect. And you might be surprised to find that the things you most worry about as a parent are the things your kids are grateful for when they grow up.

Samuel was one of nine children. His mother used to apologize to her kids for being unable to give them enough attention, but Samuel didn't see it that way when he was growing up and doesn't now. "I was always amazed at how my mother and father could focus on any one of us as individuals, but they always did," he says. "My parents attended every single sporting event and theater and music competition. Dad was my scoutmaster, and mom was my greatest fan and best friend. Having them always present meant a great deal."

Samuel's parents used to worry about providing enough because, with nine kids, the family had to be careful with money. But Samuel didn't feel deprived. "The seven boys in our family were known for showing up for any game and never having the best equipment," he says, "but hardly ever leaving without a victory."

And today, many parents would be surprised at how little attention Samuel's parents paid to grades and how much freedom their kids had. They simply required their kids to get a C average or they would have to forgo extracurricular activities. Samuel says he's still amazed at what his parents permitted him to do. And they didn't get involved with the decisions of teachers and coaches either. They wouldn't have dreamed of asking a coach to give their kid more time on the field. "They said earn it or shut up," Samuel says.

Samuel grew up in a family with limited income, time, attention, academic intensity and adult supervision. Many people might say that's a suboptimal way to raise a kid. But that's not how Samuel sees it. According to him, he grew up in a household that was bursting with love, respect and support. His parents encouraged him to use his talents, become responsible, think hard and work hard, depend on others, and be dependable in return. They gave him what he needed to create a great life for himself — and he has. Samuel has a lovely family and a high-powered executive career that capitalizes on his talents.

So what does makes a difference in your children's development? Many factors play a role. One study examined the behaviors of parents of high-achieving black middle school students. A behavior that stood out was that the parents individualized how they thought about each of their kids. They had a positive belief in their children, and they had specific ways to motivate them. Further, these parents could talk vividly about their children's talents, and 92% could list their children's unique talents.

These parents' other specific behaviors fell into six categories:

- **Direction:** Parents provided direction for their children by verbalizing their expectations, helping their children get a good education and emphasizing the importance of their children working to the best of their ability. They also modeled appropriate behaviors and were advocates for their children when necessary.

- **Concentrated time:** Parents devoted their time and effort in both learning and working situations with their children, including doing homework, spending one-on-one time, playing games, or reading and talking with them. When they were alone with their children, the parents listened to what their children wanted to talk about and discussed it with them.

- **Celebrations:** Parents celebrated with their children. They made sure their kids experienced good times by intentionally planning celebrations and positive experiences. Parents often started structuring these fun times when their children were very young.

- **Recognition:** Parents gave their children individual, generous praise and reinforcement. The recognition and rewards parents gave were directly focused on their children's achievements.

- **Emotional support:** Parents provided personal, often physical, emotional support to their children. They expressed their love in a physical manner, wanted to be available to their children and often spent time watching them perform or play. These parents also often supported their children by listening more than talking.

- **Structure:** Parents intentionally talked with their children about right and wrong at times other than when the children had done something wrong. They also put a priority on doing things neatly, correctly and orderly. Parents provided their children with opportunities to take meaningful responsibility, helped them develop their own plans and goals, conveyed responsibility by modeling, and trusted their children to be responsible.

Samuel's parents didn't know about this study when they raised their family, but he would say those bullet points describe how his parents raised him. Yet Samuel's mom felt she needed to apologize. She raised nine amazing people despite having little time or money, but she still thought she didn't parent the right way. Parents need to remember that parenting means helping their children thrive and grow, and there isn't one right way to do that.

"[Strength-based] parenting adds a **'positive filter'** to the way a child reacts to stress. It also limits the likelihood of children using avoidance or aggressive coping responses."

— Lea Waters, Ph.D., professor, Melbourne Graduate School of Education, University of Melbourne

CHAPTER FOUR

Your Parenting Strengths

In strengths-based organizations, employees can apply their talents and strengths to benefit their company in the form of positive business outcomes. They can gravitate toward careers where they find satisfaction and avoid ones where they don't. They can even receive strengths coaching and deliberately find job roles that fit and make the best use of their talents.

But that's the working world. In parenting, you don't get to do that. As a parent, you have to tailor your talents to the job of parenting. And you might often feel you're failing — full of guilt and worry. Instead of obsessing about your areas of weakness, spend more time enjoying your children. You can accomplish more if you adapt your parenting approach to fit your talents, just as some people have done with their careers.

For instance, if Restorative is one of your top Clifton StrengthsFinder themes, you're probably good at — and don't mind — fixing problems. You know that problems won't go away if you ignore them, and you've got the courage to face them. That's a valuable skill in the office, but it's also useful when your kids are having trouble in school. Or take Consistency. If Consistency is one of your top themes, you likely have a strong sense of fairness and need predictability. Your adherence to your family's "standard operating procedure" can help create and maintain rules that keep your kids safe and healthy.

Consciously understanding and using your talents and strengths and then arranging your life to make the most of them takes practice and effort. It might be difficult to find the time and energy to focus on your own talents and strengths if you have young children because their needs are immediate, constant and always changing. But the effort is worth it.

Take Felix and Anna, a two-career couple with three kids. Felix loathes clutter. He says that being in a messy house feels like someone's yelling at him. Anna doesn't really mind clutter. In fact, she admits she's more likely to make messes than to clean them up. And their kids, like all kids, are champion clutterers.

Felix and Anna took the Clifton StrengthsFinder assessment, and their results showed they have two top five themes in common (Communication and Futuristic). But Anna's top theme is Individualization, and Felix's is Discipline. Knowing what their dominant talents are gave them a new kind of mutual acceptance and understanding, Anna says.

"I think Felix always believed that I don't mind clutter because of some kind of moral weakness — that any decent person would *want* to pick up the house every day, but I don't," says Anna. "But now he gets it. I just see stuff as stuff. Stuff can be in a cupboard, stuff can be on the table, but it doesn't make much difference to me."

"And Anna understands now that to me, clutter is a sign that things are beginning to fall apart, like a leak in the ceiling that's eventually going to wreck the roof," Felix says. "When the house is a mess, all I can think of is getting it back to normal before it gets worse."

Messes give Felix a sense of impending disaster, and coping with that takes a lot of his mental and emotional energy. He would rather put his energy toward his family. Still, Anna doesn't see clutter as a problem. She really doesn't see it at all. The clutter situation was irritating them both, though, and something had to change. So Felix and Anna decided to put their strengths to use.

First, Felix, Anna and the kids drafted a "Clutter Constitution." They would all work harder at picking up after themselves, but de-cluttering the house is Felix's job because he's good at it. Anna is getting better at tidying up, but she'll never be highly organized. Because she doesn't have to spend time trying to meet Felix's expectations of a clean house, she is free to make the most of her strong Individualization talents by taking over coaching duties for their kids' teams. Sports are important in their family, and they've both always volunteered to coach their kids' teams. But Anna is better at it and enjoys it more than Felix does.

By drawing on their unique talents and strengths, Felix and Anna have made their home, their family and themselves happier. As an added bonus, because they used their talent themes as the foundation of their new daily de-clutter mission, they think about their talents more often. That's important for Felix and Anna as individuals, but it's also good for them as a team. Partners work better when they use their talents together.

The best partnerships have a super power

Felix and Anna, like many two-parent households, are fortunate to have a broad range of talents and strengths. Because you're not likely to share the same talents as your partner, together you will have a broader perspective for parenting. In fact, the odds that two people will have the same top five themes (in any order) is roughly one in

278,000. Couples who orchestrate their lives using all their dominant talents have an advantage, especially if they work together.

One of the hardest parts of parenting is the constant barrage of decisions you have to make on the spot. Whether the decisions are big or small, they all take attention. If as a couple, you let your talents guide you — "I'll figure out the carpooling schedule with my Arranger, and you find out what each of the kids wants to do this weekend with your Individualization" — you have a kind of super power.

People who collaborate well using their talents and strengths are more than the sum of their parts. Members of the best partnerships tend to say they get more and better work done together than they ever could separately. Consider these eight elements of a powerful partnership as you and your partner create your strengths-based parenting approach:

- **Complementary Strengths:** Everyone has weaknesses and blind spots that create obstacles to reaching a goal. One of the most powerful reasons for teaming up is working with someone who is strong where you are weak, and vice versa. Individuals are not well-rounded, but pairs can be.

- **A Common Mission:** When a partnership fails, the root cause is often that the two people were pursuing separate agendas. When partners want the same thing badly enough, they will make the personal sacrifices necessary to see it through.

- **Fairness:** Humans have an instinctive need for fairness. Because the need for fairness runs deep, it is an essential quality of a strong partnership.

- **Trust:** Working with someone means taking risks. You are not likely to contribute your best work unless you trust that your partner will do his or her best. Without trust, it's easier to work alone.

- **Acceptance:** We see the world through our own set of lenses. Whenever two disparate personalities come together, there is bound to be a certain friction from their differences. This can be a recipe for conflict unless both learn to accept the idiosyncrasies of the other.

- **Forgiveness:** People are imperfect. They make mistakes. They sometimes do the wrong thing. Without forgiveness, it's hard to move forward when there are misunderstandings, when communication breaks down and when partners make mistakes. And they inevitably will.

- **Communicating:** In the early stages of a partnership, communicating helps prevent misunderstandings; later in the relationship, a continuous flow of information makes the work more efficient by keeping the two people synchronized.

- **Unselfishness:** In the best working relationships, the natural concern for your own welfare transforms into gratification in seeing your partner succeed. Those who have reached this level say such collaborations become among the most fulfilling aspects of their lives.

There are hundreds of ways people can work together to raise children. Single parents can partner with friends, neighbors and grandparents. And sometimes married spouses can feel as though they are single parents — those with spouses who travel, who are in the military or who work different shifts than they do, for example.

If you feel like you are parenting alone, is there someone in your life you could partner with? Does your child have a teacher or mentor you could talk to? Could you use technology to connect with a spouse, friend or relative? All parents need the emotional support a partner can provide and someone to collaborate with.

But all parents have to collaborate with their children too. Anyone who has tried to get a toddler in a snowsuit understands that. Turning babies into happy, healthy, independent adults who can create fulfilling lives for themselves — that's the real partnership between parents and kids. And parents who know and use their strengths will have a much easier, and more fulfilling, time of it.

"**Know your kids.** Don't just know what they like, know what makes them tick. **Know what they look forward to every day** and how they express and receive love. **Know their strengths.**"

— Maggie McMahon,
entrepreneur and mother

CHAPTER FIVE

Understanding Your Children's Strengths

When parents find out they're going to have a baby, they look at their world with a whole new perspective. They'll do everything they can to keep his food, crib and clothes safe. They'll stop at nothing to provide him the best learning opportunities. And they'll monitor everything and everyone around him so the people in his life are as dedicated to his well-being as they are. Parents do all this because they love their child and want to protect him — and also because they have been told that their child's future depends on the environment he is raised in.

But does it? The answer to the nature vs. nurture question — what makes us who we are, our DNA or our upbringing? — is both. Our talents are innate, but how we express them has a lot to do with our circumstances and experiences. Obviously, children who grow up in abusive homes, in violent places or in desperate poverty have challenges to overcome that many people can't even imagine. Their upbringing teaches these children to survive, but not necessarily to thrive.

Hopefully, parents of kids born into loving homes create the optimal environment for their children, giving them what they need to grow and develop. The definition of "optimal" depends on the parents and family. Some families wouldn't dream of raising kids anywhere but on a farm, and others can't imagine their children growing up in a city without a symphony.

But all parents want the best for their children. And the best *for* a child is the best *in* the child. Regardless of the environment — with or without livestock, with or without a symphony — children will be happier and do better when they are working within their talents. So nurture the nature.

Discovering the nature, however, takes time and attention. As the executive director of Gallup's Donald O. Clifton Child Development Center, I have the tremendous pleasure of hearing our teachers talk about how the kids in their classes are growing and how their talents are emerging. One of the things we look for when selecting teachers for the center is their ability to individualize. We look for teachers who can spot emerging talents in the very young — who see possibilities and notice the uniqueness of each child.

Along with development focused on cultivating children's talents, teachers have an objectivity that parents may not have. They can step back and perceive the differences between kids and notice different levels of development. Shiloh takes a little more time than most kids do to warm up to a group, say, or Jordan is unusually quick to comfort others. To our teachers, that indicates emerging talents. To their parents, that may just be Shiloh being Shiloh and Jordan being Jordan. It's easier to see individual differences when you interact with a variety of children every day.

That's important for parents of preschool and school-aged kids to know. Teachers see children in a different setting than parents do. They are trained to look for and identify abilities and issues that may not be noticeable to parents. So ask questions and listen closely to what your kids' teachers say. Think about how their answers match up to your kids' strengths and weaknesses. Teachers have perspective, and that helps you nurture the nature.

That said, I've never met a parent who's willing to wait for a child to start school to see what her emerging talents are. Parents start looking for their children's personality traits even before they're born. And parents have been asking Gallup strengths experts for advice and assessment on children for many years.

Your children's talents

Everyone is born with certain talents. To develop those innate talents, you have to know what they are. So how can parents discover their children's natural talents?

Of course, people change over time, and the younger a person is, the more opportunity there is for change. However, though personalities evolve, scientists have discovered that core personality traits are relatively stable throughout adulthood, as are passions and interests. In fact, a 23-year longitudinal study of 1,000 children in New Zealand found that a child's personality at age 3 shows remarkable similarity to his or her reported personality traits at age 26. This research suggests that the roots of personality might be visible at an even younger age than originally thought.

Even in very young children, some dominant traits start to shine through. You may notice if your child is especially quick to make new friends, for instance, or unusually competitive — personality aspects that may hint at future strengths. One thing you can do is watch for these four indicators of budding talent:

- **Yearnings:** Your child is drawn to the same activity or environment repeatedly.

- **Rapid learning:** Your child learns a new skill or gains new knowledge quickly.

- **Satisfaction:** Your child has a sense of energizing psychological fulfillment when she takes on and meets challenges that engage her talent.

- **Timelessness:** Your child becomes so engrossed in an activity that she loses all sense of time whenever she's doing it.

When you see your child display these clues time after time, she's probably working in an area of talent.

In addition to watching your child for clues to her talent, there are formal ways to discover her talents. Gallup offers different options appropriate for your child's age, reading level and maturity level. *See the Clifton StrengthsFinder, Clifton Youth StrengthsExplorer and StrengthsSpotting sections of the book to learn more.* As a general guideline:

- If your child is 15 or older, she is likely ready to take the Clifton StrengthsFinder assessment. This is the same assessment adults take and uses concepts and terminology that adults and older children are likelier than younger children to understand. This book includes an access code that you or your older child can use to take the Clifton StrengthsFinder assessment.

- If your child is 10 to 14 years old, she should take the Clifton Youth StrengthsExplorer assessment. This assessment was specifically designed for kids in this age range. This book includes an access code to take the Clifton Youth StrengthsExplorer assessment.

- If your child is younger than 10, refer to the StrengthsSpotting section of this book. Gallup does not have a formal assessment for younger children. However, the StrengthsSpotting section will give you ideas for observing your child's potential talents, strengths and interests.

One of the best ways to understand your child's talents is to first understand your own talents. Use the shared language of strengths to familiarize yourself with the various themes of talent. Knowing your own talents and strengths increases your awareness and ability to spot and understand talents in your children.

Along with knowing your talents and observing and listening to your child, gather all the information you can. You'll soon begin to determine the traits and patterns that are your child's talents. And then you can create an environment where she can make the most of those talents and start helping her turn them into strengths.

Your child's talents may not be the same as yours

As a parent, remember that, like your interests and the activities you enjoy, your talents might be different than your child's. If Competition is in your top five themes, for example, you might have trouble understanding why your child isn't as driven as you are. Maybe he doesn't care if he wins the game, but he enjoys being with the other kids or being part of the team.

Elizabeth is a grandmother who has Empathy in her top five themes. She experiences life through emotion, she loves feeling her feelings and she pities people who don't have a rich emotional life — people like her son, her daughter-in-law and their two daughters. "Actually, I thought my son and my daughter-in-law were maybe doing something wrong with the girls," she says. "Not that my son and his wife are cold, but it seemed like they were raising the girls to be all brain, no heart."

When the girls were little, they had fun playing with dolls and watching old movies with Elizabeth. But as they got older, their activities started gravitating toward the academic. "The older one is on the chess team and math club. The other does chess and plays the viola," says Elizabeth. "Last Christmas, I told my daughter-in-law that I meant to buy the girls those books about vampires, and she said they wouldn't like them — too sappy, she said. I thought all teenagers like vampires, but I guess not."

Elizabeth was surprised — and a little hurt, she admits — by her daughter-in-law's answer. She was even more surprised at the book her family gave her for Christmas, *StrengthsFinder 2.0*. Her son works for a strengths-based company and thought she might enjoy learning something new about herself. So she took the Clifton StrengthsFinder assessment to make him happy. "As it turned out, I liked doing it, and I felt the test was pretty accurate," Elizabeth says. "My top five themes are just what I would have picked: Empathy, Connectedness, Harmony, Relator and Achiever."

And they were almost exactly what her son had picked, he told her later. He and his wife tried to guess his mom's top five themes, and they got four of them right. "Then he said the girls had taken the strengths test too. All of their themes are focused on strategic thinking and making things happen," Elizabeth says. "So I feel that these things they do — the math and music and stuff — is probably what they want to do, not what they feel they have to do. And that makes me feel better."

Leading with her Empathy talent, Elizabeth found it hard to understand her analytical son's child-rearing choices, though it was easier once she saw the strengths assessment results and realized that her granddaughters had their own talents, interests and perspectives.

More likely than not, your children will not have the same exact talents that you do. Don't assume, as Elizabeth did, that your children or grandchildren will be just like you and enjoy the same things you do. You may share some talents, or you may not have any in common. In any case, your children's talents will give you a window into their minds and hearts and an idea of what guides and motivates them as well as what activities they are drawn to.

And some parents will go to great lengths to get their children into certain activities. That's understandable. They want every option available to their kids. And children need to try a lot of different things to see what they like and what they are capable of.

But how do you know which activities — and how many — are good for your children? Are they overscheduled? Are all their activities helping or hindering their development? Is there some benefit to letting kids figure out on their own how to spend their spare time? Start by letting your children experiment with different experiences to help them see where their best path for success may be. You may be surprised where that path leads.

Would you let your child grow algae under her bed? Sara Volz says she was "born to experiment," but before she knew exactly what she wanted to do, her parents supported her many interests and let her try a variety of things — spelling bees, art clubs, theatre groups, math camps — some with more success than others. Sara even thought she would be on Broadway someday.

Sara, who is analytical and a natural learner and communicator, was always fascinated by how things worked. In sixth grade, she entered her first science fair. That's where she really found her niche for experimenting. To Sara, it was incredible that by asking a question she could test and working through difficulties to find meaningful answers, she was discovering more questions. "It was then that I knew that I was stepping — just a little ways — into the unknown," she says. "And that sent shivers down my spine."

Her science fair experiment was simple, but the experience produced "a crystallizing instant" when she knew that was her life, her dream. She wanted to be a researcher. Not knowing where it would lead, her parents gave her support and space to build on her passion and talent, including permission to set up an in-home lab in the kitchen, in the back yard and eventually, under her loft bed — where she set up her groundbreaking algae biofuel lab when she was in high school.

When Sara was a senior, she won the 2013 Intel Science Talent Search, one of the oldest and most prestigious high school science research competitions in the U.S. Her award was a $100,000 scholarship.

Her parents were thrilled with her ambition, realizing that she wanted her sports days traded in for science. Sara says, "I didn't have to worry about having their support. Some kids have that problem, but they were amazing."

People need to find what resonates with them. Sometimes that means changing activities, and sometimes it means sticking with one. When your child wants to quit something she is involved in, should you let her? It depends on your family, and it depends on your child. When your child does want to quit an activity, carefully consider what's going on. Before she gives up on the activity, think about why she wants to quit and if you think she should.

William's daughter Terry was a top-ranked high school swimmer. She almost always placed in the top spot at swim meets. And her coaches predicted that in another year, she would break the school record and qualify for state. One day, Terry told her father that she was tired of swimming and wanted to quit the team. Her father was shocked. He loved watching Terry swim and was very proud of her. Instead of telling her she couldn't quit, William considered why she might be feeling this way. Was she not getting along with the coach or other kids on the team? Was swimming taking too much time away from her new boyfriend? Were the expectations on her too high? Or was she just burned out?

In his heart, William knew that this was a bump in the road and that Terry might just need a break. He didn't want her to regret a quick decision. Knowing that she had Responsibility in her top five themes, William told Terry that it was her decision and that she didn't need to decide right away. He also told her that he knew she would be disappointed if she didn't use her swimming talents to the fullest. William knew that Terry wouldn't want to let her father, herself or the team down. And it worked. Terry stayed on the swim team and broke the school record the following year.

Kids need to learn that even with talent, it takes practice to get really good at something. However, if your child is not learning, not engaged and not improving in whatever activity she's doing, it may not get any better for her. And if she's got no natural talent for the activity and she doesn't like doing it, she may have a good reason for asking to do something else.

That's what strengths-based parenting is all about: using your talents to help you parent and teaching your kids to use their talents to help them grow. All parents want to create the optimal environment for their kids, but eventually children have to create their own environment. It will be a happier, more successful one if they start with their talents and invest time practicing, developing skills and building knowledge to turn their talents into strengths.

"Our greatest contribution is to be sure there is **a teacher in every classroom who cares** that every student, every day, learns and grows and feels like a real human being."

— Donald O. Clifton, Ph.D. (1924-2003),
Father of Strengths-Based Psychology

CHAPTER SIX

Strengths-Based Schools

When I was growing up, my dad gave a lot of speeches around our state — mostly commencement speeches. Some of my best memories were when he would take me along. He was a great speaker, and I always took a lot of pride in watching the responses and ovations from the audience. Before each speech, he would ask me which stories he should share with the audience. I always urged him to include "The Animal School," a fable created in the 1940s by George Reavis. Dad added his own flair to it; his version went something like this:

Imagine a meadow with some young animals — a duck, fish, squirrel and rabbit. These animals decided that they wanted to have a school, just like people. So with the help of some grown-up animals, they built their school. They put together a very practical curriculum that would have running, swimming, jumping, tree climbing and flying — courses that would make them well-rounded animals.

On the first day of school, the little rabbit combed his ears and went hopping off to his first class, running. There he was a star. He ran to the top of the hill and back as fast as he could go, and, oh, did it feel good. He said to himself, "I can't believe it. At school, I get to do what I do best." His teacher said, "Rabbit, you really have talent for running. You have great muscles in your rear legs. With some training, you will get more out of every hop." The rabbit thought, "Oh, I just love school! I get to do the things I like to do and then learn to do them better."

The next class was swimming. The rabbit said, "Wait. Rabbits don't like to swim. I don't want to be here." The teacher replied, "You may not like it now, but five years from now, you will know it was a good thing for you." The rabbit was pretty sure that was not true and that he would not like swimming.

In tree-climbing class, a tree trunk was set at a 30-degree angle so all the animals had a chance to succeed. Even though the rabbit tried very hard, he didn't get very far. But he did better than some of the other animals, so he would probably pass tree climbing.

In jumping class, the rabbit did just fine. But in flying class, he had problems. So the teacher gave him a test and discovered he belonged in remedial flying. In remedial flying class, the rabbit had to practice jumping off a cliff. The teacher said he could learn to fly if he wanted to and worked hard enough at it.

The fish had a great deal of difficulty with running, but the squirrel got along just fine. Like the rabbit, he didn't like swimming. Because he struggled with it, he was placed in a swimming class with the rabbit. In tree climbing, the squirrel was fantastic. He could jump from branch to branch easily and go through the trees magnificently. In jumping, the squirrel was above average. Flying was a problem for the squirrel, so they put him in the rabbit's class.

The duck showed early signs of delinquency. She couldn't get her stride in running. She was very competitive, so when she was behind, she would use her wings and start flying in order to win. But in the manual, it said that animals with wings were not to use them during running. The duck insisted on using her wings every time she got behind, so they put a clip on her wings. That frustrated her, so she quacked when she was supposed to be quiet, and they told her to stop quacking. And then she bit another animal.

Then one day in tree climbing, when the duck had to climb along with the rabbit, the rabbit got ahead of her and she lurched forward and ripped the web out of her feet. That hurt. She just flew to the top of the tree, which was again the wrong method. They yelled at her to come back, but she flew away. That confirmed that they had a delinquent duck on their hands.

In the fourth week of school, the rabbit was developing his talent for running. It felt good. The teacher recognized the rabbit's excellence in running and told him that he was looking forward to some great running performances. The rabbit felt great and wondered why he had ever spent time in the meadow when he could have so much fun learning and excelling in running.

When the rabbit went back to swimming class, the instructor said that the animals would jump in the water. "Wait, wait," said the rabbit. "I talked to my parents. They didn't learn to swim. We don't like to get wet. I'd like to drop this course." The teacher said, "You can't drop it. The drop-and-add period is over. Either you jump in or you flunk."

So the rabbit jumped in. He panicked! He went down once. He went down twice. Bubbles came up. The instructor saw he was drowning and pulled him out. The other animals had never seen anything as funny as this wet rabbit who looked more like a rat without a tail, and they laughed at him. The rabbit was more humiliated than he had ever been in his life. He wanted desperately to get out of class. He was glad when it was over.

Then the rabbit went to tree-climbing class, and he took a big run at the tree because he wanted to show what he could do. Still wet from swimming class, he slipped off the tree and hurt his leg, so he didn't do well in jumping that day either. In flying, he got right to the edge of the cliff where he was supposed to jump, and he couldn't do it. He rolled down the side of the cliff and went home dirty.

When he got home, he told his parents he was not going back to school. He thought that his parents would understand and help him. He told them, "I don't like school. I just want to be free." His parents said, "If the rabbits are going to get ahead, you have to get a diploma." The rabbit didn't want a diploma. They argued. They made him go to bed, and he didn't sleep well that night. He struggled to get out of bed the next morning and didn't even comb his ears.

He went off to school that day with a slow hop. Then he remembered the counselor saying that any time he had a problem, her door was always open. So he hopped up on the chair by the counselor and said, "I don't like school." He told the counselor that he did not want to be in swimming, he did not like to get wet and he really liked running. He told her about the day the instructor said he had to jump in the water or flunk, how humiliated he was, how he rolled down the cliff and had to go home dirty.

The counselor said, "Rabbit, I hear you saying you do not like school because you don't like swimming. But swimming is what you really need to work on. I see you have been doing very well in running. So I don't know why you need to work on running. What you need is to work on swimming. I'll arrange it so you don't have to go to running anymore, and you can have two periods of swimming."

When the rabbit heard that, he just threw up.

Student engagement

Children start school full of excitement about what they will learn, what they will get to do and how they will shine. They are fully engaged and eager to be there. But what happens over time? Gallup knows from surveying more than 3 million students in elementary through high school that engagement levels are highest in elementary school, take a downward turn in middle school and continue this trend into high school.

One of the key findings from a recent survey of 600,000 students is that those who strongly agree that their school is committed to building the strengths of each student and that they have at least one teacher who makes them excited about the future are 30 times as likely to be engaged at school as their peers who strongly disagree with both statements. What if schools prioritized talent exploration and engagement in the learning process?

Children need exposure to a variety of activities and educational opportunities. They won't know if they're great at something if they don't know it exists. Imagine if Shaun White was never taken to a ski slope, if Taylor Swift wasn't given a guitar, if Elon Musk had not had access to a computer. Kids do need to be exposed to lots of different things — but they don't need to be good at everything.

Yet the myth of well-roundedness is that they *should* be good at everything. This is especially noticeable in education. You name it — reading, sports, math, leadership and sociability — schools require and expect children to do well in all areas. Like the rabbit in the story above, having shown promise at snowboarding, Shaun White should have focused on poetry. Taylor Swift should have started concentrating on chemistry even though she had musical talent. And

Elon Musk should have pushed the keyboard aside and put a lot more time into tennis. Sounds absurd, doesn't it?

Considering that your child will spend a tremendous portion of his life in school, strengths-based schools and educators are not just a bonus. When schools take a strengths-based approach, they begin by identifying and developing educators' and students' strengths. Focusing on what is right with learners and educators creates classroom discussions and teaching and learning strategies that lead to academic success.

There is also compelling evidence to suggest that kids' engagement in school and in the learning process relates directly to academic performance. The results of a study of 78,106 students across eight states revealed dramatic results. A one-point increase in student engagement was associated with a six-point increase in reading achievement and an eight-point increase in math achievement scores.

Selecting schools

When your kids go off to school — kindergarten, high school, college — what do you want? Sure, you want them to get good grades, be involved in activities and generally excel at everything they are offered. But what you really send them to school for is what all parents ultimately want for their children: better lives. You want your children to become thriving adults with high well-being who are engaged in work that is meaningful to them.

When parents begin the search for the right school for their children, they start with "all of them" and hope to end with "exactly the right one." One of the questions they often ask is whether a private or public school is better. Private schools or home schooling may be better for instilling certain values. Public schools are prohibited from religious evangelizing, for instance. And if you teach your children at home, they'll learn what matters most to you.

But when selecting a high school, middle school, grade school or preschool that will put your child on a positive path, it isn't whether it is public or private or how large or small it is that matters most to your child's long-term engagement and well-being. What matters is teachers, mentors, school leadership, projects, internships and extracurricular activities. Knowing that may have important implications for the decisions you make when selecting schools.

Teachers play a major role in your child's development, but you don't always get to choose the teacher. You are more likely to be able to choose which school your child attends. And because your child will likely be at the same school for several years, your challenge is to find the school with the best teachers. You will also want to consider school leadership, programs, engagement levels and achievement measures.

How can you find the best school for your child? Become an informed investigator:

- Start by talking to other parents who have children in the school. Ask about their experiences with teachers. How many teachers do they describe as outstanding? Does the school have a reputation for having several great teachers?

- Listen for specific information about teachers from students and parents. In particular, listen for these key points:

  - the teachers' individual attention to children

  - teachers who are sensitive to student needs

  - teachers who come up time after time because of their positive relationships with students and parents

  - teachers who communicate regularly with parents through text, email or personal notes

- Ask about the school's principal. Gallup has found that principals are incredibly important to a child's learning experience. According to a 2013 Gallup report, great principals:

  - have high expectations, set goals for the school and present a vision for the school

  - work hard for teachers and encourage innovation

  - are in classrooms often, help teachers use their strengths and treat teachers as individuals

  - like to be with students, are liked by students, understand what is best for students and make decisions based on what is best for students

  - celebrate success, encourage teachers to celebrate, and believe that recognizing success improves performance and the school

  - are optimistic about the future, see problems as opportunities and believe success can come from negative experiences

  - welcome parents to feel like they are part of the school, inspire parents to support teachers, and help parents and teachers focus on what is right for students

- Investigate the school overall and how it fits in the community.

  - Does the school show high engagement scores for teachers and students? Many schools publish results on their district websites.

  - Ask about special programs such as art, music or sports that appeal to your child. Has the school received recognition for its special programs?

- Does the school have a variety of ways to involve parents? Some schools have evening or weekend sessions to teach parents about new programs, and some have regular social events to help parents feel welcome at the school.

- Look at the school's achievement scores on its website. Are they strong or improving?

- Does the school promote and offer different ways for students to get involved and excel?

- Does the school offer numerous extracurricular activities?

- Do students have the opportunity to work on long-term projects or internships?

Teachers, school leadership, programs, engagement levels and achievement measures are important at the K-12 level. There are also other factors to consider for your child's future as he moves beyond high school. *The 2014 Gallup-Purdue Index Report*, which includes interviews with more than 30,000 U.S. college graduates, found that what matters most about college — as it applies to long-term workplace engagement and personal well-being — are six critical elements related to experiential and deep learning as well as emotional support.

Graduates' odds of being engaged at work and thriving in all areas of well-being are higher if:

1. they had an internship or job that allowed them to apply what they were learning in the classroom

2. they were extremely active in extracurricular activities and organizations while attending college

3. they worked on a project that took a semester or more to complete

4. they had at least one college professor who made them excited about learning

5. their college professors cared about them as a person

6. they had a mentor who encouraged them to pursue their goals and dreams

Looking for teachers who have the talent to teach

Adults remember their great teachers — the ones who taught them more than they thought they could learn and who opened doors they didn't even know were there. Teachers like that are immensely valuable, and I'm pleased to have had the opportunity to observe and work with not only teachers at the Child Development Center, but also many teachers and administrators in schools all over America. I have seen firsthand the difference these professionals make. A good school can do a lot for a child, but a good teacher does a whole lot more.

Good teachers have a tremendous long-term positive effect on children — longer than you might realize. A recent study found that great teachers not only raise their students' test scores, but their students are likelier to go to college and earn a higher income, and they are less likely to become teenage mothers.

A 2012 Phi Delta Kappa/Gallup poll asked Americans: "Please think about the teacher who has had the most positive influence in your life. Thinking about that teacher, please tell me three words or phrases that best describe how that teacher made a difference." The top three responses were "caring," "encouraging" and "attentive/believed in me." That's how adults remember their own best teachers and what you as a parent might look for in your child's teachers.

While you want your child's teacher to be caring and attentive, it's also important to look for a teacher who is effective and who has the talent to teach. It's easy to see modern technology and updated classrooms when visiting a school, but it's harder to see teacher effectiveness and talent. Good teachers are naturally gifted at spotting and encouraging their students' emerging talents. And Gallup's research has found that teachers with extreme talent for the role also share three important qualities that might not be evident during a school tour:

- They have a strong drive to see their students achieve.

- They establish learning environments centered on close relationships.

- They promote an innovative and individualized yet ordered classroom structure.

What do schools look for in effective teachers? According to a 2014 Gallup-*Education Week* survey of K-12 superintendents, when evaluating a teacher's performance:

- Nearly all superintendents say overall teaching effectiveness (96%) and the level of student engagement (94%) are very important factors.

- Almost eight in 10 superintendents (79%) say feedback of the principal and the learning growth of students (78%) are very important factors. Thirty percent say feedback of fellow educators is very important.

- Few say student test scores (16%) or the number of years of experience in the classroom (6%) are very important factors.

So even though students, parents and superintendents might all look for different qualities in teachers, adults' memories of their best teachers and superintendents' assessments of their best teachers both describe teachers who help students grow, learn and develop.

Parents want a teacher who is engaged

Maria has two elementary-age girls, and she was looking for a new school for them. Her kids have been in one parochial school and three different public schools. Maria used her Strategic, Input and Activator talents to find the best environment for her children. She considered all of her options and gathered as much information as possible. When she did find one she liked, she pounced.

"I knew right away that this was the right place," Maria says. "There was a kind of happy energy as soon as I walked in the door, and the principal, Dr. Gomez, met me immediately. He wasn't looking for me. He was talking to a student, but he came right up and introduced himself."

Maria began asking questions on the spot. She asked him about engagement, strengths, and how he handles state tests and teacher union issues. She even asked about his philosophy of parking for pick up and drop off. Maria liked what she heard.

"It seemed like he was *all* about teachers and kids. Dr. Gomez was super excited about kids learning and about what his teachers were doing. And it seemed like he knew specifically what *every* teacher was doing," Maria says. "So I told him all about my girls and enrolled my younger daughter for the next year and put my older daughter on a waiting list. Then I drove home thinking I'd like to work for that guy."

But Maria wasn't happy about the teacher her daughter got the next school year. "For a second-grade teacher, Ms. Silver seemed pretty hard, even harsh," Maria says. "And my girl is bubbly and goofy and emotional. I thought her teacher was going to crush her, so I went straight back to Dr. Gomez."

The principal heard Maria out, but he didn't pull Maria's daughter out of Ms. Silver's class. Instead, he cautioned Maria to wait. "Dr. Gomez said to give it time and to watch my daughter closely," Maria says. "He'd transfer her to another teacher at the semester if I still wanted to, but he wouldn't do it now."

So Maria, fearing the worst, kept an eye on her daughter. She expected her daughter to become deflated and sad and that her learning would suffer. But it didn't. Instead, she blossomed. "She became a little less goofy. But she talked and talked and talked about Ms. Silver and what she was learning. She even invented homework for herself, which she brought to Ms. Silver, who treated it seriously," Maria says.

"Eventually, I figured out that my daughter was trying to make her teacher proud or that Ms. Silver was making my daughter proud, one or the other," says Maria. "Something about that woman made my girl want to succeed. I didn't understand it at first, but there was a dynamic there that was really good for my daughter. The principal was right."

What he knew and Maria didn't was that Ms. Silver had the talent to recognize and encourage each student's unique qualities. She quickly related to every child and discovered what motivated each of them, how they learned best and what they were interested in. Those are the qualities parents want in their child's teacher. Parents want a teacher who is engaged and who engages students; who helps students learn the material for real, not just for a test; and who helps kids develop their talents into strengths.

The parent-teacher partnership

No matter who your child's teacher is, create a partnership with him or her. This partnership is especially important if your child and his teacher aren't clicking. That's when parents really need to use their strengths to advocate for their kids.

Set up a meeting, ask questions, listen closely and apply your talents and strengths. For example, if you have Input, do your research and bring relevant facts, data and ideas to the meeting. If you have Command, speak candidly and directly about sensitive subjects and move discussions forward by removing obstacles. If you have Harmony, focus on practical matters, look for consensus and smooth ruffled feathers if necessary. Keep in mind, however, that the deficit-based model that influences much of the educational system might be a hurdle you have to overcome. Teachers are often charged with remedying deficits. But assume that your child's teacher wants to do more.

Explain why your child does what he does. Kids with strong social themes aren't talking all the time because they're bored or disobedient; they're just psychologically compelled to connect. They are the type of students who will thrive when they are learning with a small study group or participating in a group project. It may be difficult to get kids with strong themes such as Focus to transition. It's not because they're stubborn. It's because they can't bear to stop before they're finished.

Kids with a theme like Organizer are uncomfortable when they feel uninformed. My friend Karin got a call from her daughter's teacher who was annoyed because Karin's daughter insisted on reading the teacher's lesson plan every day. Karin had to explain that her daughter wasn't looking over her teacher's shoulder; it's just that the little girl needed to know what to expect so she could organize her things, her time and her expectations. And she felt a lot better if she knew the agenda for her day, every day.

Explaining a child's psychological motivation to her teacher can help the teacher understand the child. Teachers want to motivate children. It helps them teach better. Motivation is a significant aspect of learning.

In *NurtureShock*, Po Bronson and Ashley Merryman point to the work of Silvia Bunge for why we need to understand what motivates individuals. Bunge says, "Motivation is crucial. Motivation is experienced in the brain as the release of dopamine. It's not released like other neurotransmitters into the synapses, but rather it's sort of spritzed onto large areas of the brain, which enhances the signaling of neurons." They continue, "The motivated brain, literally, operates better, signals faster. When children are motivated, they learn more."

Kids are going to struggle in some areas. But assume that your child has talents that can help her manage her weaknesses so they don't create learning barriers. For instance, remember Anthony and Camil? They finally recognized that their daughter's orientation toward routine could help her keep track of her things, despite her inclination toward disorganization. But it took years to come to that realization, and they've known her since the minute she was born.

Teachers don't have the advantage of knowing a student the way a parent does. On the other hand, they do have the advantage of spending a lot of time studying the fundamentals of development and learning. So partner with your child's teacher by openly and honestly sharing your insights and observations. And listen objectively to the teacher's observations as well.

Many schools have hired and developed talented educators, identified the strengths of each teacher and student, and created engaging learning environments. When I'm in one of those schools, I often see students' and teachers' top talent themes printed on cards and taped to classroom doors, and it reminds me what a great environment a strengths-based school can be. Not only are these teachers in tune with how to use their strengths in the best interest of the students, but when parents know a teacher's strengths, it gives them tremendous insight into the inner workings of the classroom. It also makes it faster and easier for parents and teachers to build partnerships that facilitate growth.

Moving mountains

Generations ago, parents didn't go to such lengths to get their kids in certain schools with certain teachers. Times have changed, and they'll keep changing. One thing that won't change, however, is the need for children to learn and to know how to apply what they've learned. That doesn't mean everyone needs to take the same educational route, but every child needs to grow up to be a productive part of his or her world.

If your child is not in a strengths-based school, strengths-based parenting is even more important. In *Ready or Not, Here Life Comes*, Dr. Mel Levine clearly states, "Schools teach many of the general competencies with the sometime support of parents. Mothers and fathers have to lead the way in helping kids discover their personal affinities, those sometimes partially concealed pockets of talent that can develop into passions and areas of expertise, to say nothing of careers."

If your child's school focuses more on what he does wrong than what he does right, you will need to do some extra navigation. If his teachers don't understand or support his strengths and help him manage his weaknesses, share your perspective. Parents have the advantage of seeing each of their children as unique and talented.

They should be guardians of that talent, holding it in high regard and supporting its evolution. It can be hard to resist spending time on what is wrong and on areas of lower performance. Instead, focus your energy on adjustments you need to make to chart a course for your child's educational future guided by his strengths. He'll be more engaged now, and he'll have a greater sense of well-being later.

No matter where a child goes to school, parents can be a driving force behind education. Nancy, a former principal, says, "Parents are so powerful … they don't realize that they are the customers and have essentially purchased their child's education and thus are partners in focusing on what their child does best. A lobby of smart parents is a great principal's dream team to move a school in the right direction and to reset meaningful targets. If a teacher doesn't lead with what is going well, parents need to ask. When parents stay involved and positive, their child's potential is more likely to be attained."

Parents will move mountains for their children. Talented teachers, principals and school leaders nourish young people's strengths. They unearth their hopes and dreams and weave them into their educational goals. As Nancy said, "Parents are so powerful." Remember that, and use your strengths to help move mountains so schools prioritize the principles of talent exploration and engagement in the learning process.

"The real task of parenting is not to prepare the path for our children — rather, to **prepare them for the path they will inevitably need to walk.**"

— Wayne Hammond, Ph.D.,
CEO, Resiliency Initiatives

CHAPTER SEVEN

Belief, Support, Appreciation

So much in society tells you that you need to have a certain lifestyle or be just like some other parent who used some other method that you should incorporate right away or else you will fail your children. And there is an expectation for children and parents to be well-rounded — to be good at everything.

But everyone has different talents and strengths. Think about other parents you know — moms on the bleachers, dads at PTA meetings, parents at your workplace, your neighbors and your best friends. Which one of you likes to organize field trips? Who likes to speak up at group meetings? Who isn't afraid to bring up difficult topics? Who is the peacemaker for the adults, and who is the peacemaker for the kids? You don't have to play all those roles. You don't have to be a well-rounded parent, and you don't have to have well-rounded kids.

But you do need to know how to make the most of your talents and strengths. And you do need to figure out how to encourage your children as you use your own natural tendencies to appreciate, support and build on their individuality.

A life lived in strengths

Terrell was always a good student, but he was especially good at math. His parents nurtured that ability any way they could. His dad gave him his old bookkeeping textbooks. His mom bought him the most up-to-date calculator and got him workbooks from the school supply store.

Terrell enjoyed math, but that was only one part of the childhood he describes as "really happy." He played sports and music; visited his grandmother every Sunday; and went fishing with his dad, uncles and cousins. He learned how to take care of a lawn, a friendship, a job — all the stuff of a typical American boyhood. "There wasn't a lot of money," Terrell says, "but I had a fantastic childhood. Sometimes we butted heads, but I always had a very supportive household."

But when Terrell was 14, on Thanksgiving Day, his father died.

Suddenly his mother became a single parent. It was up to her to support her family financially and emotionally. She needed to fortify herself and find her inner strength. That's more than enough for anyone to deal with.

Terrell's mom went back to school and back to work. She was passionate about healthcare and realized that nursing was how she could best support her family financially, and it was also something she could do well. "She became the president of various state and national nursing associations and was a co-founder of the teachers union in our hometown," Terrell says. "Mom taught me the importance of education and getting involved in any endeavor you thought was worthwhile, even though it meant a lot of traveling and work for her. She didn't believe in just sitting on the sidelines."

And not sitting on the sidelines also meant she lobbied to get Terrell into advanced math, English and writing classes. She took him to piano, drum and trumpet lessons. She rarely missed his ballgames, and on days when Terrell carried the team, she talked to him about being humble and thankful for his opportunities. She encouraged Terrell and his friends, and she trusted him to do a good job. "I can't remember a time when she hounded me about my homework," Terrell says. "She trusted that I would just do it. And I did."

Terrell grew up, went to college, launched a career and had a family of his own. And he clearly sees his parents' influence on the life he created. "My kids are well-educated, and they have pride in their education, careers and families," Terrell says. "But when we're together, we always eat around the table and talk, just like when I was a kid."

Terrell's mom might have had an easier life if her husband hadn't died unexpectedly, if her job hadn't required her to travel or advance her education, if her son hadn't wanted to be involved in time-consuming extracurricular activities, or if she had let the schools take charge of his education and let others take care of teacher and nurse associations. Perhaps, but Terrell's mother had talents that compelled her to get involved — to make the world better. As she built a life around her passions, not only was she a role model, but she also helped Terrell grow from his interests and strengths.

Everything she did must have taken tremendous energy and will, but it was likely easier for her to do it than to "sit on the sidelines." I admire Terrell and his mom, and I'm glad his mother lived a life that capitalized on her talents and strengths and that she encouraged her son to do the same. It was good for her, good for her son and good for her community.

There are many people like Terrell's mother who make the world better by using their talents and strengths. Sometimes they make a small part of the world better — a place no bigger than the family home. Sometimes they make a huge part of the world better, and we all benefit. In either case, a life well-lived is a life lived in strengths.

Shaping the future

I was talking with a young woman named Isabella recently who, after two years of marriage, is contemplating starting a family. But Isabella is afraid — afraid of all the scary things that could happen to a child and afraid she won't be the right kind of parent. I was about to tell her, "Oh, it'll be fine" and dismiss her concerns. She's a smart, capable 30-year-old who has a job she loves, a husband she adores and a comfortable home to raise a child in. But instead I asked, "What are you afraid of?"

She told me about her childhood, her parents, her siblings, her foster families and the rough world she grew up in and the people who should have been there for her but weren't. I began to understand her insecurity about raising a child. Isabella feels lucky to have made it out of a world of drugs and abuse; her stepbrothers and stepsisters didn't. She's thoughtful and wants to be responsible about bringing a child into the world.

So I asked her, "How did you get where you are now from where you started?" Isabella didn't hesitate. "My grandma. She was always there for me, and I spent a lot of weekends with her. She believed in me and helped me know who I am and how to find my path. She supported me and helped me define my values and beliefs." Isabella always knew that her grandmother appreciated her as an individual.

When she was with her grandmother, she didn't feel stressed. She could just enjoy being with someone who valued her.

When children know that they are special to someone, it builds their resiliency. And that someone is typically an adult — a parent, grandparent or teacher who lets them know they are important and unique. For Isabella, that adult was her grandmother. And because of that relationship, Isabella not only persevered, but she became resilient. That resiliency helped her overcome her background, and she became the kind of person who can make a life that she chooses.

She's scared about becoming a parent because she had so few role models for parenting. But she had one — her grandmother. One person taught Isabella that she's worthy, that she's capable and that she has strengths. That's what Isabella needed to know as a child. And that's what Isabella needs to know before having one.

So that's what I told her. I told her that she's a good person and that she can be a good parent — that she has talents and strengths she has already put to use as a student, as a spouse and in her work life. She can use those same strengths as a parent.

No matter how subtle or dramatic the differences are, we each grow up under different conditions and environments. While there isn't a prescription for what each parent and each child must do to have a life well-lived, understanding your own unique constellation of talents as well as your children's gives you a course to chart that fits your parenting, fits your children and fits your family.

There are millions of people from all walks of life and from all over the world who are living better, healthier and happier lives because someone recognized what was unique in them. Someone taught them that they do better when they focus on what comes naturally to them. Parents should be among those millions of people. Our job as parents is to nurture our children's nature, to be detectives and discover who our children already are and who they are becoming, to be coaches and create pathways that play to their strengths and manage their weaknesses. As parents, we should have the tools and knowledge to build strong families. When we raise children who know their talents and build them into strengths, we shape a better future.

The key to strengths-based parenting:

---

1 Know and understand your own talents and how you can best apply them with your children and family.

2 Discover your children's talents and help them develop their talents into strengths.

The Language of Strengths

As a parent, you strive to understand and communicate with your children. Sometimes you connect with them. Sometimes you misunderstand each other and have to try again. Sometimes words have one meaning to you and a different meaning to your children. But a common language can facilitate communication and mutual understanding. The language of strengths can clarify and help you better comprehend your own talents and your children's talents by defining what makes you and your children wonderfully unique.

Because everyone has a distinctive set of talents, people see the world through their own personal filters, or lenses, from the time they are born. Their culture, upbringing, extended families, education, what they see and read, work and life experiences, travel, friends, and peers influence their perceptions. And people make judgments about what they see and hear because of the unique lens they are looking through. For instance, through one person's lens:

- An act of caring might be labeled as good.

- Telling a joke during school might be labeled as bad.

- Thinking about the future might be labeled as valuable.

- Getting upset about losing a baseball game might be considered overreacting.

Another person who looks at the same situations through his unique lens might say it's a social talent to tell a joke at school or it's a natural part of competitiveness to get upset about losing a game. Everyone has his or her own way of looking at the world.

As you familiarize yourself with the different themes of talent and start to recognize your own talents, you will become increasingly aware and able to recognize your children's talents. The next three sections of the book will help you identify and learn more about your talents and your children's talents using the language of strengths. Each section includes valuable information and action items for you and your children. Refer to the Clifton StrengthsFinder section to learn more about your own talents and strengths. Then, consult the appropriate sections based on the age and maturity level of your children.

Clifton StrengthsFinder:

- Recommended age level: Parents and children 15 and older

- Clifton StrengthsFinder assessment (access code to take assessment included with this book)

- 34 themes of talent

Clifton Youth StrengthsExplorer:

- Recommended age level: Children aged 10-14

- Clifton Youth StrengthsExplorer assessment (access code to take assessment included with this book)

- 10 themes of talent

StrengthsSpotting:

- Recommended age level: Children younger than 10
- No assessment; refer to book content
- Uses the 10 Clifton Youth StrengthsExplorer themes of talent as a foundation

When people take the Clifton StrengthsFinder assessment and see their dominant talents, they often say it is a revelation *and* something they already knew. Likewise, many of your children's talents may be familiar, and some might surprise you. You're almost certain to see talents you could have predicted but in a whole new light.

While identifying your talents and your children's talents is an important first step, it takes investment — time spent practicing, developing your skills and building your knowledge base — to develop those talents into strengths. The more you and your children think about and understand these talents, the more you will be able to recognize opportunities to develop them into strengths. The more your talents are developed into strengths and put into action, the happier and more energized you and your children will be.

Clifton StrengthsFinder

93

Recommended age level:
Parents and children 15 and older

Clifton Youth StrengthsExplorer

233

Recommended age level:
Children aged 10-14

StrengthsSpotting

277

Recommended age level:
Children younger than 10

Achiever	Futuristic
Activator	Harmony
Adaptability	Ideation
Analytical	Includer
Arranger	Individualization
Belief	Input
Command	Intellection
Communication	Learner
Competition	Maximizer
Connectedness	Positivity
Consistency	Relator
Context	Responsibility
Deliberative	Restorative
Developer	Self-Assurance
Discipline	Significance
Empathy	Strategic
Focus	Woo

Clifton StrengthsFinder

All people have a unique combination of talents, knowledge and skills — strengths — that they use to do their work, achieve their goals and interact with others every day. Gallup has found that when people understand and apply their strengths, the effect on their lives is transformational. People who use their strengths every day are *six times more likely to be engaged in their work and three times more likely to say they have an excellent quality of life.*

Yet, many people don't even know what their talents are or have the opportunity to build them into strengths. In fact, many people spend their lives focused on fixing their weaknesses instead. The Clifton StrengthsFinder is an online assessment that helps people identify their talents and build them into strengths. The assessment identifies 34 themes of talent — areas where an individual's greatest potential for building strengths exists. By exploring how you naturally think, feel and behave, the Clifton StrengthsFinder identifies the areas where you have infinite potential to grow and succeed.

In 2001, Gallup introduced the original Clifton StrengthsFinder assessment in *Now, Discover Your Strengths*. The book's author and creator of the assessment, Dr. Donald O. Clifton (1924-2003), was named the Father of Strengths-Based Psychology by the American Psychological Association. In 2007, Gallup published *StrengthsFinder 2.0* and unveiled a new and upgraded version of its popular assessment.

For decades, the Clifton StrengthsFinder has helped people excel and realize the benefits of leading with their strengths — from top business executives and managers to salespeople, nurses, teachers, students, pastors and others. And Gallup has published more than half a dozen books focused on strengths-based development in various roles. All of these books have used the Clifton StrengthsFinder as the cornerstone of strengths discovery and personal improvement. The Clifton StrengthsFinder is the culmination of more than 50 years of Dr. Clifton's lifelong work, which has led to more than 12 million people worldwide discovering their strengths.

TAKING THE ASSESSMENT
Recommended age level:
Parents and children 15 and older

This book includes an access code that you or your older child can use to take the Clifton StrengthsFinder assessment. This unique code is in the packet in the back of the book. After you complete the assessment, you'll receive a report that lists your top five themes of talent and have access to materials and tools to help you better understand your unique talents.

Your top five theme definitions will be customized to you, based on your unique combinations of responses during the assessment. Each of the 34 Clifton StrengthsFinder themes also has a standard theme definition. As you examine your top five talent themes in greater detail, read this section for each theme's standard definition, action items for you or your child, and questions to consider for strengths development.

People exceptionally talented
in the Achiever theme work
hard and possess a great
deal of stamina. They take
immense satisfaction in being
busy and productive.

Achiever

Your Achiever theme helps explain your drive. Achiever describes a constant need for achievement. You feel as if every day starts at zero. By the end of the day you must achieve something tangible in order to feel good about yourself. And by "every day" you mean every single day — workdays, weekends, vacations. No matter how much you may feel you deserve a day of rest, if the day passes without some form of achievement, no matter how small, you will feel dissatisfied. You have an internal fire burning inside you. It pushes you to do more, to achieve more. After each accomplishment is reached, the fire dwindles for a moment, but very soon it rekindles itself, forcing you toward the next accomplishment. Your relentless need for achievement might not be logical. It might not even be focused. But it will always be with you. As an Achiever you must learn to live with this whisper of discontent. It does have its benefits. It brings you the energy you need to work long hours without burning out. It is the jolt you can always count on to get you started on new tasks, new challenges. It is the power supply that causes you to set the pace and define the levels of productivity for your work group. It is the theme that keeps you moving.

If you have **Achiever**

- Make sure that parenting is on your daily to-do list. Use the stamina this theme provides to help you stay in the marathon of parenting. There is no greater accomplishment than raising great kids.

- When you are working hard to get a job done, invite your children to join you so they can see what hard work involves.

- Create a to-do list for yourself that includes activities in areas that are important to your children. For example, you could join committees for their school, athletic or music groups.

- Remember that your drive for hard work might be more intense than it is for other people and that you might not need as much rest as they do. This awareness will help you accept when your children or other family members approach work less intensely than you do.

- Help your children identify the most important facts, concepts or ideas they learn in school each week. This will help you chart their learning progress, and you will feel like you and your children are moving forward.

If your child has **Achiever**

- Suggest that your child join groups or clubs that have specific goals and that get real results. He will enjoy belonging to organizations that accomplish goals rather than those that just talk about them.

- Share your to-do list with your child, and ask what is on his list each day or week. Consider how you could help him complete his list if he invites you to. Ask him questions to help him prioritize activities. Are there any projects you could do together?

- Understand that children haven't had as much experience managing time, school, work, projects or other activities as adults have. The desire may be there, but you might need to clear the path for your child to make his way through his to-do list.

- At the end of every day, point out your child's successes. At the end of each week, ask him about his achievements, and appreciate and recognize them. Help him become more aware of his accomplishments, and let him know that you noticed.

- Consider how you can showcase your child's accomplishments: a wall of photos; a portfolio; a list of daily, weekly or monthly achievements; or a refrigerator display. At each age and stage, find ways to display his success.

Questions for strengths development

What specific goals are you working toward?

Could you partner with other hard workers at school or work to accomplish something this week?

What is one challenge you are currently facing at school, work or home? What steps are you taking to overcome it?

Do you remember to celebrate your achievements before moving on to the next challenge?

People exceptionally talented

in the Activator theme can

make things happen by

turning thoughts into action.

They are often impatient.

Activator

"When can we start?" This is a recurring question in your life. You are impatient for action. You may concede that analysis has its uses or that debate and discussion can occasionally yield some valuable insights, but deep down you know that only action is real. Only action can make things happen. Only action leads to performance. Once a decision is made, you cannot not act. Others may worry that "there are still some things we don't know," but this doesn't seem to slow you. If the decision has been made to go across town, you know that the fastest way to get there is to go stoplight to stoplight. You are not going to sit around waiting until all the lights have turned green. Besides, in your view, action and thinking are not opposites. In fact, guided by your Activator theme, you believe that action is the best device for learning. You make a decision, you take action, you look at the result and you learn. This learning informs your next action and your next. How can you grow if you have nothing to react to? Well, you believe you can't. You must put yourself out there. You must take the next step. It is the only way to keep your thinking fresh and informed. The bottom line is this: You know you will be judged not by what you say, not by what you think, but by what you get done. This does not frighten you. It pleases you.

If you have **Activator**

- Use your Activator talents to make sure your children don't miss out on critical opportunities. You naturally act on their behalf and can help them clarify their preferences by pushing them to try something new.

- Tell your children about times when you acted quickly and how it worked out, for better or worse. Sharing your experiences will give your children snapshots that show the consequences of various actions they can consider when they face similar situations themselves.

- You like to get things going, so volunteer to be in charge of group discussions with other parents. You can help people move beyond just talking by steering them toward the next step.

- When your children have a problem to solve, look for opportunities to help them speak out or become part of the action. By involving your children, you can lead them to faster and more effective outcomes.

- When you have insights or great ideas, record them for your children so you can act on them at the proper time. This will help you feel like you are moving forward, even though you might have to wait before taking action.

If your child has **Activator**

- Tell your child that you know she is great at initiating. Ask her how to get things moving in her groups of friends, teams or your family. Your expectations will energize her.

- At parent-teacher conferences, explain that your child likes to make things happen, and ask her teachers to give her action-oriented activities and responsibilities. By communicating your child's Activator talents, you can increase her opportunities to use them — and to stay motivated.

- Encourage your child to take responsibility for her intensity. Reinforce that even when she is part of a group, she shouldn't hesitate to ask for action. Her Activator talents can compel others to get going in the right direction.

- Sometimes the inner urgency and impatience your child feels can be perceived as negative or disruptive. Talk with her about the power of her Activator talents and how she can channel her action-oriented energy most productively.

- When your child complains, listen carefully — you may learn something. Talk about how she can make improvements or take initiative for change. Do this quickly because, unchecked, a child with Activator may stir up negativity and get off track.

Questions for strengths development

What is something you initiated or moved forward this week? How did that make you feel? How did those around you react?

What is your system for getting things going? Who or what helps you take action quickly?

When you are in a group, are you often the one who asks others to take action? Do they take action? How do you get others to start moving in a positive direction?

How can you help others move their great ideas from concept to implementation?

People exceptionally talented

in the Adaptability theme

prefer to go with the flow.

They tend to be "now" people

who take things as they come

and discover the future one

day at a time.

Adaptability

You live in the moment. You don't see the future as a fixed destination. Instead, you see it as a place that you create out of the choices that you make right now. And so you discover your future one choice at a time. This doesn't mean that you don't have plans. You probably do. But this theme of Adaptability does enable you to respond willingly to the demands of the moment even if they pull you away from your plans. Unlike some, you don't resent sudden requests or unforeseen detours. You expect them. They are inevitable. Indeed, on some level you actually look forward to them. You are, at heart, a very flexible person who can stay productive when the demands of work are pulling you in many different directions at once.

If you have **Adaptability**

- Appreciate your natural talent for flexibility. Living with children is surprising and unpredictable. You will thrive in this changing environment.

- Embrace each moment of being a parent. You seldom see the needs of your children as inconvenient distractions.

- Be aware of the value of your talent when the pressure is on. Your ability to quickly adjust to changing demands can soothe and give confidence to your children, who might freeze under pressure.

- Understand that others might prefer structure to spontaneity. Explain to your children that your love for spontaneous situations helps you make the most of each moment as it presents itself.

- Remember that sometimes, your children might not realize the advantages of making changes — to schedules, chores or rules. Share your natural insights in this area. Help them understand how your willingness to adjust can benefit them.

If your child has **Adaptability**

- Your child is at his best when he can react and respond. When considering classes and projects, remember that he will likely be most productive on short-term assignments that require immediate action.

- Encourage your child to join clubs and teams. Remind him that his flexibility can make a positive difference in any group. When things don't go as planned, he will be able to adjust to the new circumstances and move forward.

- Your child may need your support making choices that are in his best interest. Be sensitive as you help him realize that sometimes he may need to say no to complete his priorities. Ask questions or offer scenarios that allow him to practice adapting quickly.

- Suggest that your child increase the variety in his weekly schedule. He will be most productive when his school and work activities offer multiple challenges.

- Remind your child that there is a reason things seem to just fall into place. Make sure he realizes that this is a result of his special ability to adjust to changing circumstances, rather than pure luck. Thank him for his flexibility.

Questions for strengths development

What do you need to do today? What do you need to respond to today?

How can you use your ability to adapt to reassure friends, family and coworkers when they get upset by changing circumstances?

Whom can you partner with to help you plan your long-term goals?

How did you use your flexibility today? What happened? How did things work out?

People exceptionally talented

in the Analytical theme

search for reasons and

causes. They have the ability

to think about all the factors

that might affect a situation.

Analytical

Your Analytical theme challenges other people: "Prove it. Show me why what you are claiming is true." In the face of this kind of questioning some will find that their brilliant theories wither and die. For you, this is precisely the point. You do not necessarily want to destroy other people's ideas, but you do insist that their theories be sound. You see yourself as objective and dispassionate. You like data because they are value free. They have no agenda. Armed with these data, you search for patterns and connections. You want to understand how certain patterns affect one another. How do they combine? What is their outcome? Does this outcome fit with the theory being offered or the situation being confronted? These are your questions. You peel the layers back until, gradually, the root cause or causes are revealed. Others see you as logical and rigorous. Over time they will come to you in order to expose someone's "wishful thinking" or "clumsy thinking" to your refining mind. It is hoped that your analysis is never delivered too harshly. Otherwise, others may avoid you when that "wishful thinking" is their own.

If you have **Analytical**

- Help your children make sense of the complexities of life by objectively talking through the pros and cons of various situations and decisions they need to make.

- Parenting can often be emotional. Use your naturally impartial perspective to bring reason and objectivity to emotional situations with your children.

- Your ability to look for patterns can be an asset as you partner with your children's teachers. For example, at parent-teacher conferences, gather clues to understand how your children could learn more. Or, try to figure out the teachers' teaching talents and how they translate to your children.

- When situations arise that confuse or upset your children, help them understand the circumstances by asking questions, explaining logically what happened and sharing your objective opinion.

- When your children are putting together a campaign or project, help them by gathering information or pointing out patterns that might be a key to success. Especially when your children are struggling with a seemingly overwhelming project, you can bring structure to their ideas.

If your child has **Analytical**

- You may not always agree with your child, but be sure to take her point of view seriously. Chances are good that she has thought things through very carefully.

- Accuracy is important to your Analytical child. Getting a project or assignment done right might be more important to her than meeting the deadline. Check in with her to ensure that she has a deadline in mind and adequate time to complete the project.

- When you explain a decision you have made to your child, remember to share your reasoning. Even if you feel you are overexplaining, lay out the logic clearly. People with Analytical talents appreciate objectivity. Whether your child agrees or not, she will respect your decision more.

- Ask your child to help you with decisions about family or work situations. When you ask for her opinion, you give her opportunities to practice and refine her thinking. And you show her that you recognize and respect her analytical thought process.

- Explain your child's Analytical talents to her teachers. Ask them to explain their reasoning to her. This will satisfy her need to know and prepare her teachers to teach her more effectively.

Questions for strengths development

What websites, books or people do you rely on as credible sources?

Whom do you like to talk with about analyzing data and finding patterns?

Who might benefit from information and facts you know?

Did you ask someone a question today? Did you get a good answer? What did you conclude from the answer?

People exceptionally talented

in the Arranger theme

can organize, but they

also have a flexibility that

complements this ability.

They like to determine

how all of the pieces and

resources can be arranged for

maximum productivity.

Arranger

You are a conductor. When faced with a complex situation involving many factors, you enjoy managing all of the variables, aligning and realigning them until you are sure you have arranged them in the most productive configuration possible. In your mind there is nothing special about what you are doing. You are simply trying to figure out the best way to get things done. But others, lacking this theme, will be in awe of your ability. "How can you keep so many things in your head at once?" they will ask. "How can you stay so flexible, so willing to shelve well-laid plans in favor of some brand-new configuration that has just occurred to you?" But you cannot imagine behaving in any other way. You are a shining example of effective flexibility, whether you are changing travel schedules at the last minute because a better fare has popped up or mulling over just the right combination of people and resources to accomplish a new project. From the mundane to the complex, you are always looking for the perfect configuration. Of course, you are at your best in dynamic situations. Confronted with the unexpected, some complain that plans devised with such care cannot be changed, while others take refuge in the existing rules or procedures. You don't do either. Instead, you jump into the confusion, devising new options, hunting for new paths of least resistance and figuring out new partnerships — because, after all, there might just be a better way.

If you have **Arranger**

- Parenting involves juggling multiple realities, which likely is easier for you than it is for others. Make the most of your natural flexibility and talent to manage unpredictable circumstances to alleviate stress for your children and family.

- Use your Arranger talents to coordinate your children's efforts. With creative planning, you can decrease their dependence on you and increase their independence.

- Even the best arrangements or routines can be more efficient. Challenge yourself to find ways to improve and streamline your children's schedules or activities.

- Get involved with other parents who share your interests and who are involved in your children's activities. Learn these parents' talents so you can help them match their talents to the tasks at hand.

- When you rearrange schedules or activities, remember to tell your children, family, friends or other groups why you are making adjustments. They may need to understand your reasons to appreciate why you are making changes.

If your child has **Arranger**

- Arrangers are resourceful. Give your child projects or jobs that require this talent. When something is not working, let him figure out other ways to do it.

- Let your child take responsibility for planning the family's weekly menu or everyone's chores for the week.

- Help your child prioritize his homework according to deadlines and how much each assignment affects the final grade. Arranging and aligning priorities will help him plan for maximum efficiency and benefit.

- Encourage your child to help teachers and school administrators plan projects and special occasions, such as school dances or homecoming celebrations. He will enjoy making the most of all the moving parts, alternatives and quick changes that go into organizing big events.

- Remember that your child is at his best when he is involved and busy. Arrangers thrive when they have a lot going on because that is when their natural ability to juggle multiple demands really kicks in.

Questions for strengths development

What activities or events do you like or want to plan?

What do you like best about pulling all the pieces together?

What activities or clubs are you involved in now? How can you help others in these groups become more efficient? How can you become more efficient yourself?

How can you rearrange or configure your room, desk or workspace for maximum effectiveness?

People exceptionally talented

in the Belief theme have

certain core values that are

unchanging. Out of these

values emerges a defined

purpose for their lives.

Belief

If you possess a strong Belief theme, you have certain core values that are enduring. These values vary from one person to another, but ordinarily your Belief theme causes you to be family-oriented, altruistic, even spiritual, and to value responsibility and high ethics — both in yourself and others. These core values affect your behavior in many ways. They give your life meaning and satisfaction; in your view, success is more than money and prestige. They provide you with direction, guiding you through the temptations and distractions of life toward a consistent set of priorities. This consistency is the foundation for all your relationships. Your friends call you dependable. "I know where you stand," they say. Your Belief makes you easy to trust. It also demands that you find work that meshes with your values. Your work must be meaningful; it must matter to you. And guided by your Belief theme it will matter only if it gives you a chance to live out your values.

If you have **Belief**

- Preach what you practice, and practice what you preach. Teach your children your beliefs, ethics and principles through your actions and words. They will see and hear your core values as you live them out every day.

- Actively seek roles that fit your values. Think about joining organizations that define their purpose by the contributions they make to your children, family and community.

- List your top beliefs on a piece of paper and use it as a bookmark or post it somewhere you will see it. Clarifying your beliefs and keeping them top of mind will help you live by and develop them. In living your beliefs, you serve as an example to your children.

- Give voice to your beliefs in a way that is comfortable for you. Help your children know what you value and why you value it. Talk about right and wrong from your perspective. By sharing your beliefs, you can inspire your children and clarify concepts that might be fuzzy for them.

- Values are more "caught" than taught. Find moments every day to show and tell your children what is important to you and your family.

If your child has **Belief**

- Tell your child not to be afraid to talk about and take pride in what she believes in. Owning and expressing her values can help others know who she is, what she stands for and how to relate to her.

- Peers can challenge a young person's belief system. Watch for times when your child needs help dealing with others who don't share her values. Peer pressure is powerful, and your child might need additional support addressing it.

- Share with your child what you value and why you value it. Talk about right and wrong with her. Listen to her, and respect her point of view. Discussing her beliefs with you can help her refine and develop them and give them breadth and depth. She will appreciate your interest.

- Help your child find opportunities to express her values and put her beliefs into action — volunteering at a hospital, joining a campaign team, mentoring younger children or applying for an internship. Aligning with others who have a similar mission can energize her and satisfy her sense of purpose and conviction.

- Encourage your child to actively seek friends who share her basic values and who enjoy discussing them. Spending time with these friends will be affirming for her and will help her develop and solidify her principles.

Questions for strengths development

Have you ever written down your core values? What comes to mind first?

Who has influenced your beliefs? How?

How do your beliefs guide your decisions? Do others ever challenge your beliefs? What do you say when they do?

What are the beliefs of people you admire? Do your friends and the people you spend the most time with share your values?

People exceptionally talented

in the Command theme have

presence. They can take

control of a situation and

make decisions.

Command

Command leads you to take charge. Unlike some people, you feel no discomfort with imposing your views on others. On the contrary, once your opinion is formed, you need to share it with others. Once your goal is set, you feel restless until you have aligned others with you. You are not frightened by confrontation; rather, you know that confrontation is the first step toward resolution. Whereas others may avoid facing up to life's unpleasantness, you feel compelled to present the facts or the truth, no matter how unpleasant it may be. You need things to be clear between people and challenge them to be clear-eyed and honest. You push them to take risks. You may even intimidate them. And while some may resent this, labeling you opinionated, they often willingly hand you the reins. People are drawn toward those who take a stance and ask them to move in a certain direction. Therefore, people will be drawn to you. You have presence. You have Command.

If you have **Command**

- Children can be vulnerable. Be strong on your children's behalf to increase their security and reduce their fear.

- You tend to voice thoughts that others might not dare express. Your willingness and need to provide clarity can be an asset for groups your children belong to. Consider which groups need your Command and when to use it to benefit your children and others.

- Show your children that it is possible for a person to be strong and forceful without being a bully.

- You have the courage to say no. Use your natural ability to be upfront to set an example for your children and for other parents.

- Strengthen your relationship with your children by speaking plainly and directly, yet tactfully, about sensitive subjects. Approach these discussions thoughtfully. Your willingness to face the truth can give your children confidence and security.

If your child has **Command**

- Encourage your child to join groups that need help selling and/or raising money for school projects. Help him refine his Command talents by talking with him about ways to get others to contribute.

- To develop your child's Command talents into strengths, notice and reinforce the words, tones and techniques he uses that have the potential to change confrontation into real persuasiveness.

- Support your child in finding a cause to believe in and champion. You might discover that he is at his best when defending a cause in the face of resistance.

- Tell your child to look for classes with instructors who love to debate ideas and problems and who encourage such debate. He will enjoy these exchanges. And when others are shy, nervous or uncomfortable, his example can give them confidence to express their ideas.

- Let your child know that many of his peers may not have the Command talents he does. Tell him that by listening to others, he can be an encouraging voice for their ideas and thoughts and an advocate on their behalf.

Questions for strengths development

What are you in charge of at school, work or home? What do you like about being in charge?

Have you persuaded anyone lately? About what? How did you persuade them?

Did you speak up for anyone today?

Did you share your opinion with anyone today?

People exceptionally talented

in the Communication

theme generally find it

easy to put their thoughts

into words. They are

good conversationalists

and presenters.

Communication

You like to explain, to describe, to host, to speak in public and to write. This is your Communication theme at work. Ideas are a dry beginning. Events are static. You feel a need to bring them to life, to energize them, to make them exciting and vivid. And so you turn events into stories and practice telling them. You take the dry idea and enliven it with images and examples and metaphors. You believe that most people have a very short attention span. They are bombarded by information, but very little of it survives. You want your information — whether an idea, an event, a product's features and benefits, a discovery, or a lesson — to survive. You want to divert their attention toward you and then capture it, lock it in. This is what drives your hunt for the perfect phrase. This is what draws you toward dramatic words and powerful word combinations. This is why people like to listen to you. Your word pictures pique their interest, sharpen their world and inspire them to act.

If you have **Communication**

- Create the oral tradition of your family using vivid words and anecdotes that will help your children relive defining moments.

- Share stories with your children and their friends. Your animated tales can bring adults and kids together and keep relationships and communication open. Be sensitive about which stories that involve your children and family you tell and whom you share them with.

- Tell your children about your workday or your other activities. You create pictures and vivid ideas through vignettes that help your children understand who you are, what you do and how you handle different situations.

- Apply your Communication talents when your children are struggling to find the right words. Whether they are working on a school project, planning a presentation or don't know what to say to a friend or teacher, use your way with words to help them craft an effective message.

- When you notice that your children are getting bored with a project, chore or activity, use your entertaining side to create fun and moments of humor. You can help change your children's outlook by being productively entertaining.

If your child has **Communication**

- Take time to ask about and listen to your child's stories about school, activities and friends. She will enjoy telling you, you will enjoy listening and it will deepen your relationship. Make sure to really listen to what she says.

- It is easy for your child to carry on a conversation. Encourage her to use this natural gift as a way to draw others in, especially those who are new to a group.

- Find platforms for your child to give speeches or presentations to groups. Help her hone her Communication talents by listening and watching her practice. Let her know that her ability to describe and explain can clarify topics for others and give them a real lift.

- Make note of words that your child uses to get attention, and point them out to her. Help her practice these and other words she could use and different ways to convey them. This will keep her communication interesting, regardless of the material. You will also boost her self-esteem by showing her that you're paying attention.

- Ask your child if she would like to join extracurricular groups such as speech clubs or debate teams. She will thrive in verbal environments, and they offer her a good opportunity to develop her talents into strengths.

Questions for strengths development

When you talked to people today, did you notice how they reacted to what you said? Did you capture their attention or get them to laugh?

Who are your best listeners at school or work? Why do you enjoy talking with them?

Did you collect any stories to practice and perfect telling this week? What is your favorite story you told recently?

How could you use your Communication talents to foster dialogue among your friends and family?

People exceptionally talented

in the Competition theme

measure their progress

against the performance of

others. They strive to win first

place and revel in contests.

Competition

Clifton
StrengthsFinder

Competition is rooted in comparison. When you look at the world, you are instinctively aware of other people's performance. Their performance is the ultimate yardstick. No matter how hard you tried, no matter how worthy your intentions, if you reached your goal but did not outperform your peers, the achievement feels hollow. Like all competitors, you need other people. You need to compare. If you can compare, you can compete, and if you can compete, you can win. And when you win, there is no feeling quite like it. You like measurement because it facilitates comparisons. You like other competitors because they invigorate you. You like contests because they must produce a winner. You particularly like contests where you know you have the inside track to be the winner. Although you are gracious to your fellow competitors and even stoic in defeat, you don't compete for the fun of competing. You compete to win. Over time you will come to avoid contests where winning seems unlikely.

If you have **Competition**

- You probably won't find a parenting contest, but don't let that keep you from comparing yourself to someone you think is a great parent.

- Be careful not to let your children become your proxy in competitions, but take pride in their successes.

- Use your Competition talents on your children's behalf. Create your own challenges in the context of their activities. There's nothing wrong with striving to be the best coach of the soccer team, the most attentive parent on the field trip or the one who brings the best cookies to the school bake sale.

- Help your children see their wins. You naturally notice their moments of victory and successful interactions, even when they might not.

- Make your home more fun by creating contests out of everyday tasks. Share the "scoreboard" you keep with your children and family. You can motivate them — especially those who don't keep score — by showing them their successes that you have tracked.

If your child has **Competition**

- Turn your child's ordinary tasks into competitive games. He will have fun while getting chores completed, and you will both get more done this way.

- Remember, your child likes to measure his personal achievements. Create and encourage experiences that challenge him but that also result in him being successful. He might not be able to discover how good he can be without competing.

- Reinforce your child's competitive nature, and find others who do too. For example, at parent-teacher conferences, tell your child's teachers that he thrives on competition. Ask them to encourage him to always score in the top 5% of the class or to give him other competitive goals. Not only will this make his classes fun, it can motivate him and increase his learning.

- Suggest that your child compete against himself, and encourage him to top his last performance. Challenge him to make the next paper better than the last and the next grade higher than the one before.

- When your child loses, he may need to sulk, cry or punch a pillow. Don't deny those feelings. Let him give them voice, then talk it over. After that, start looking ahead to the next opportunity to win. If he loses repeatedly, he may stop playing.

Questions for strengths development

What scores matter the most to you? What scores are you currently keeping track of?

Whom do you like competing against?

What contests are you in? Did you "win" today?

What do you want to be the best at this week? How will you know if you are the best?

People exceptionally talented

in the Connectedness theme

have faith in the links among

all things. They believe there

are few coincidences and

that almost every event

has meaning.

Connectedness

Things happen for a reason. You are sure of it. You are sure of it because in your soul you know that we are all connected. Yes, we are individuals, responsible for our own judgments and in possession of our own free will, but nonetheless we are part of something larger. Some may call it the collective unconscious. Others may label it spirit or life force. But whatever your word of choice, you gain confidence from knowing that we are not isolated from one another or from the earth and the life on it. This feeling of Connectedness implies certain responsibilities. If we are all part of a larger picture, then we must not harm others because we will be harming ourselves. We must not exploit because we will be exploiting ourselves. Your awareness of these responsibilities creates your value system. You are considerate, caring and accepting. Certain of the unity of humankind, you are a bridge builder for people of different cultures. Sensitive to the invisible hand, you can give others comfort that there is a purpose beyond our humdrum lives. The exact articles of your faith will depend on your upbringing and your culture, but your faith is strong. It sustains you and your close friends in the face of life's mysteries.

If you have **Connectedness**

- Share your global perspective with your children to help them become aware of things that are bigger than and beyond themselves.

- Help each member of your family see the connections among their talents, actions, missions and successes. When people believe in what they are doing and feel like they are part of something bigger, it enhances their motivation and commitment to achieve.

- Keep a journal. Collecting and clarifying your thoughts can help you connect your ideas about what really matters to you. Share your discoveries with your family.

- Help your children cope with seemingly unpredictable and unexplainable events, and help them find meaning. Your Connectedness talents can bring comfort and valuable perspective during rough times.

- Talk to your children about what each family member values most and what your family stands for. What can you, as a family, do to take responsibility for your neighborhood, community or culture?

If your child has **Connectedness**

- Create a calm environment for your child to study, work on projects and solve problems. She needs this sense of peace, and it enhances her ability to think.

- Encourage your child to join service-oriented school and community groups. Her Connectedness talents will thrive in these environments, and they can inspire her to see the far-reaching impact of her service to others.

- Ask your child to create a list of familiar examples that support her sense of connection. Suggest that she share them with others. Her examples might help other people see connections in their own lives.

- Help your child collect articles, videos, music and illustrations that represent and demonstrate how we are all connected. Find a place in her room or in your home where she can gather and display symbols of things that are meaningful to her.

- Point out to your child times when you have seen her make sense of seemingly unpredictable or unexplainable events. Show her how her understanding helps others when they are struggling. At different stages and ages, help her put her thoughts into words and actions that will make a difference for others.

Questions for strengths development

What are one or two of your beliefs? Did you share your beliefs with anyone today?

Have you ever talked to your friends or coworkers about how they fit into the big picture?

What is your sense of purpose in life?

Whom do you admire? What does he or she believe in?

People exceptionally talented

in the Consistency theme are

keenly aware of the need to

treat people the same. They

try to treat everyone with

equality by setting up clear

rules and adhering to them.

Consistency

Clifton
StrengthsFinder

Balance is important to you. You are keenly aware of the need to treat people the same, no matter what their station in life, so you do not want to see the scales tipped too far in any one person's favor. In your view this leads to selfishness and individualism. It leads to a world where some people gain an unfair advantage because of their connections or their background or their greasing of the wheels. This is truly offensive to you. You see yourself as a guardian against it. In direct contrast to this world of special favors, you believe that people function best in a consistent environment where the rules are clear and are applied to everyone equally. This is an environment where people know what is expected. It is predictable and evenhanded. It is fair. Here each person has an even chance to show his or her worth.

If you have **Consistency**

- Use your belief in the power of consistency to create an equitable and efficient family environment. Be sure to give reasons for the rules that are applied to each family member.

- Consider volunteering as a referee or umpire in your children's sports. The community will appreciate your contribution, and you will enjoy using your talents to promote fairness.

- Create a list of examples that illustrate the value of consistency. Share the list with your children. Use these examples to help them see the positive outcomes and stability that consistency and uniformity provide.

- Your Consistency talents can give your children security and clarity, especially when they have attainable expectations. Use your talents to guide them, and give them choices with various outcomes.

- Help your children gain a sense of accomplishment. Show them how they can achieve and do well within the set parameters of their classes or extracurricular activities.

If your child has **Consistency**

- Set up a study area and a predictable study schedule for your child. This will reinforce the regularity that feels so good to him. He will be at his best when his schedule doesn't change much.

- Help your child look for ways to level the playing field. At school, church, clubs or other activities, encourage him to take the lead in providing disadvantaged people with the platform they need to fulfill their true potential.

- Your child can be a "watchdog" for social justice. What people or causes in your neighborhood, school or community might need help and more attention in this area? Give him ideas about how he could play a role in these situations.

- Be aware that your child may be frustrated by those who don't play by the rules or who don't apply the same rules to everyone. Encourage him to find classes and activities with routine procedures and practices. Support him when he asks questions and seeks justice when rules aren't applied consistently.

- When you make decisions for your child or adjust rules, be sure to explain to him why there may be variations and how it is still fair for each situation. This will give him a sense of objectivity and help him feel that any adaptations you make are unbiased.

Questions for strengths development

What rules do you live by?

Do you treat all your friends, coworkers and family members the same? How do you make sure you do? Do they know why or how you do it?

How does it make you feel when people are treated unfairly? What can you do to increase equality?

Where do you see examples of fairness around you? Which teachers, coaches or leaders have demonstrated consistent rules and behaviors? How do they show they are fair and unbiased?

People exceptionally talented

in the Context theme enjoy

thinking about the past. They

understand the present by

researching its history.

Context

You look back. You look back because that is where the answers lie. You look back to understand the present. From your vantage point the present is unstable, a confusing clamor of competing voices. It is only by casting your mind back to an earlier time, a time when the plans were being drawn up, that the present regains its stability. The earlier time was a simpler time. It was a time of blueprints. As you look back, you begin to see these blueprints emerge. You realize what the initial intentions were. These blueprints or intentions have since become so embellished that they are almost unrecognizable, but now this Context theme reveals them again. This understanding brings you confidence. No longer disoriented, you make better decisions because you sense the underlying structure. You become a better partner because you understand how your colleagues came to be who they are. And counterintuitively you become wiser about the future because you saw its seeds being sown in the past. Faced with new people and new situations, it will take you a little time to orient yourself, but you must give yourself this time. You must discipline yourself to ask the questions and allow the blueprints to emerge because no matter what the situation, if you haven't seen the blueprints, you will have less confidence in your decisions.

If you have **Context**

- Record and document your children's lives so you can remind them who they are and where they came from.

- Strengthen your family's identity by sharing stories from the past. Your stories and those of your ancestors not only give your children a glimpse of the past, they solidify family values, relationships and memories.

- Ask your children's teachers about themselves, their histories and their goals for education. Knowing where they are coming from will help you feel more connected to them and to your children's education.

- When you change plans, make decisions, share information or apply rules, explain to your children *why* you are doing what you are doing. You naturally think about the context of your actions anyway. Giving your children some background will help them better understand your motivation as well.

- When you make plans or have discussions with your children, talk about past scenarios. Use your Context talents to help your children learn from previous successes and mistakes.

If your child has **Context**

- At parent-teacher conferences, let your child's teachers know that she learns best when she has the history behind what she is learning or why she is being asked to do something.

- Suggest that your child interview people who have lived through important times in history. Have her take notes on the interviews or record them. She might want to collect and keep what she learns, and her curiosity about the past will help preserve important events and ideas.

- Ask your child if she would like to join clubs where she can collect and archive facts and memories. The school's yearbook staff, for example, might be able to use her natural talents for looking back.

- Look for organizations that could use your child's help strengthening their culture via folklore. Cultural, ethnic or religious groups might appreciate her natural talent to research and collect symbols and stories that represent the best of their past.
- Encourage your child to explain to you or others why she is doing something a certain way. Her explanation will add clarity to what she is doing, and she will be more likely to persevere.

Questions for strengths development

What friends, teachers or coworkers do you like to talk with about history? How does discussing the past with them stimulate your thinking?

What is your favorite thing to learn from or about the past? What is your best way to learn about the past?

How can examining completed projects or case studies help you be successful in the present?

Do you ask people about their backgrounds when you meet them? How does that help you get to know them better?

People exceptionally talented

in the Deliberative theme are

best described by the serious

care they take in making

decisions or choices. They

anticipate obstacles.

Deliberative

You are careful. You are vigilant. You are a private person. You know that the world is an unpredictable place. Everything may seem in order, but beneath the surface you sense the many risks. Rather than denying these risks, you draw each one out into the open. Then each risk can be identified, assessed and ultimately reduced. Thus, you are a fairly serious person who approaches life with a certain reserve. For example, you like to plan ahead so as to anticipate what might go wrong. You select your friends cautiously and keep your own counsel when the conversation turns to personal matters. You are careful not to give too much praise and recognition, lest it be misconstrued. If some people don't like you because you are not as effusive as others, then so be it. For you, life is not a popularity contest. Life is something of a minefield. Others can run through it recklessly if they so choose, but you take a different approach. You identify the dangers, weigh their relative impact and then place your feet deliberately. You walk with care.

If you have **Deliberative**

- You aren't likely to err on the side of giving too much recognition. So be aware that when you do praise your children, they will appreciate it because you give careful consideration to why and when you do. Make an intentional effort to acknowledge accomplishments that are important to your children. More specific praise from you could result in more positive actions and achievements from your children.

- Your ability to see risks ahead of time can help prevent problems. Take pride in knowing that your careful vigilance keeps your children out of harm's way and ultimately prevents unnecessary pain and sorrow.

- If you see something you know is dangerous — broken playground equipment or a street that needs a lower speed limit — report it to the relevant authority. You'll feel better.

- Have confidence in your own judgment. Always do what you think is sensible, regardless of the impact on your popularity with other parents or with your children.

- Help your children think through their decisions. You see things others don't. You can be a valuable sounding board, especially when you ask questions and listen.

If your child has **Deliberative**

- Tell your child that when he is taking a test, he should try to concentrate first on the questions he is confident answering. This will give him a sense of security as he carefully proceeds.

- Your child is likely to be most successful in class when he knows the teacher's expectations. Help him discover teachers who are best at providing clear goals.

- Have confidence in your child's judgment. Trust him to do what he thinks is right even if it means it will affect his popularity.

- When you ask your child a question, remember to give him time to respond before jumping in too quickly with your response or the next question.

- When your child is considering which extracurricular activities to join, advise him to begin with those he is most interested in. Then encourage him to talk to others, ask questions or go to a meeting before he decides. This will help him narrow his decision down to which ones are the best fit for him and will feel like a good use of his time.

Questions for strengths development

How would others describe you? Do they see you as a serious and careful person?

What is your process for making decisions? How do you identify risks?

Did you help anyone make a decision today? How do you help others think through options and come to a conclusion?

What do you expect to do today? Do you know what your teachers, coaches or coworkers expect from you?

People exceptionally talented

in the Developer theme

recognize and cultivate the

potential in others. They

spot the signs of each small

improvement and derive

satisfaction from evidence

of progress.

Developer

You see the potential in others. Very often, in fact, potential is all you see. In your view no individual is fully formed. On the contrary, each individual is a work in progress, alive with possibilities. And you are drawn toward people for this very reason. When you interact with others, your goal is to help them experience success. You look for ways to challenge them. You devise interesting experiences that can stretch them and help them grow. And all the while you are on the lookout for the signs of growth — a new behavior learned or modified, a slight improvement in a skill, a glimpse of excellence or of "flow" where previously there were only halting steps. For you these small increments — invisible to some — are clear signs of potential being realized. These signs of growth in others are your fuel. They bring you strength and satisfaction. Over time many will seek you out for help and encouragement because on some level they know that your helpfulness is both genuine and fulfilling to you.

If you have **Developer**

- Take pride in knowing that you are content to let your children be children. You realize that time is essential to their growth and development.

- Remember to develop yourself. Always have one or two mentors of your own, and meet with them frequently. They can help you understand and develop your own talents so you can help your children learn and grow.

- If you are a sports fan, volunteer to coach your children's sports teams. Your Developer talents can combine with your athletic skills and knowledge to create coaching strengths.

- Make a list of all the times you have helped your children learn and grow and of the positive effect you had on their development. Look at the list often, and remind yourself of the powerful influence you have on your children.

- Look for growth in your children's lives and tell them about it. Be specific about what you see. Your detailed observations will boost their confidence and enhance their development.

If your child has **Developer**

- Encourage your child to become a mentor or tutor. Point out specific ways she has helped other people grow or learn. Ask her if she would like to teach classes or music lessons to younger students or coach sports teams.

- Because your child is compelled to see the best in people, she might have trouble realizing when they are struggling or in the wrong role. Help her understand that sometimes, the best way to develop others is to help them move on to something else.

- Reinforce the idea that encouraging others to stretch and excel makes a difference. Tell your child that her encouragement and confidence give people the spark they need.

- Talk with your child about specific people she might like to teach or train. The opportunity to develop and support another person will be very fulfilling to her.

- Ask your child to think about her personal mission. Show her how to connect her mission with her Developer talents to make a meaningful difference in other people's lives.

Questions for strengths development

How do you know when others are succeeding? What do you say to encourage them?

Have you recognized or praised anyone recently?

Have you taught anyone something new this week? Who needs your assistance with a skill, project or activity?

What do you like best about helping others? Who has helped you grow?

People exceptionally talented

in the Discipline theme enjoy

routine and structure. Their

world is best described by

the order they create.

Discipline

Your world needs to be predictable. It needs to be ordered and planned. So you instinctively impose structure on your world. You set up routines. You focus on timelines and deadlines. You break long-term projects into a series of specific short-term plans, and you work through each plan diligently. You are not necessarily neat and clean, but you do need precision. Faced with the inherent messiness of life, you want to feel in control. The routines, the timelines, the structure, all of these help create this feeling of control. Lacking this theme of Discipline, others may sometimes resent your need for order, but there need not be conflict. You must understand that not everyone feels your urge for predictability; they have other ways of getting things done. Likewise, you can help them understand and even appreciate your need for structure. Your dislike of surprises, your impatience with errors, your routines and your detail orientation don't need to be misinterpreted as controlling behaviors that box people in. Rather, these behaviors can be understood as your instinctive method for maintaining your progress and your productivity in the face of life's many distractions.

If you have **Discipline**

- Use your Discipline talents to bring order and structure to your children's world. When you do, the certainty of predictability replaces fear of the unknown.

- Create routines for your children and family that require everyone to follow through. Over time, they will appreciate these expectations and the results they produce.

- Don't hesitate to check in with your children to ensure that things are getting done. They will come to rely on your quality checks and anticipate what they still have left to do.

- Clutter annoys you. Create a system for dealing with clutter as a family that will help you and everyone feel more in control.

- Tell your children that you can accomplish more with timelines and structure. Describe how you feel when you don't have a strong sense of order. Explaining how important these details are to you will help your children understand you and your actions better.

If your child has **Discipline**

- Give your child advance notice of changes, schedules or deadlines. He probably prefers to get things done sooner rather than later, and he can do that only when timelines are clear.

- Remember that while your child needs to prioritize, especially when there is a lot to get done, the process can be overwhelming. Take the time to prioritize together by talking through what needs to be done first and what will take the most time.

- Provide your child with roles and responsibilities that have structure. He can get more done when he does not have to try to bring order out of disorder.

- Encourage your child to talk with teachers before starting assignments. Ask teachers about their expectations and grading system. Your child will feel most comfortable when he knows what to expect and what others expect from him ahead of time.

- Help your child's teachers understand that he may need to check in about assignments or upcoming projects. This isn't because he is questioning or challenging the teacher, but rather because he needs to get it right.

Questions for strengths development

How do you like to have your day structured? How does a sense of order help you have a great day?

What routines have you put in place recently? How have they made your life more effective?

Have you helped or tried to help someone get organized lately? What places at home, school or work need less "clutter"?

How do errors and surprises make you feel? What do you do when you encounter them?

People exceptionally talented

in the Empathy theme can

sense other people's feelings

by imagining themselves in

others' lives or situations.

Empathy

You can sense the emotions of those around you. You can feel what they are feeling as though their feelings are your own. Intuitively, you are able to see the world through their eyes and share their perspective. You do not necessarily agree with each person's perspective. You do not necessarily feel pity for each person's predicament — this would be sympathy, not Empathy. You do not necessarily condone the choices each person makes, but you do understand. This instinctive ability to understand is powerful. You hear the unvoiced questions. You anticipate the need. Where others grapple for words, you seem to find the right words and the right tone. You help people find the right phrases to express their feelings — to themselves as well as to others. You help them give voice to their emotional life. For all these reasons other people are drawn to you.

If you have **Empathy**

- You naturally recognize and appreciate the emotional implications of life. Let your children know that you understand and value their experiences and individuality. When you acknowledge your children's feelings first, you can support their next steps more quickly.

- You innately sense the feelings of others and respond appropriately. Use your Empathy talents and experience to help your children learn how to deal with different emotional scenarios.

- Be the barometer of feelings for your children and family. You notice when someone is feeling left out, sad, excited or proud, and you can give others a heads up about how to respond. Share your observations of others' emotions to strengthen the bonds of trust and friendship.

- Help your children understand emotions and how you and others express them. While it is easy for you to identify feelings, it might not be as easy for your children. Sometimes, you might need to explain how certain actions or words make others feel.

- For you, emotions are just as real as more practical factors. When you interact with your children, family, neighbors or organizations, use your ability to consider all the feelings and facts so you can reach the best outcome for everyone involved.

If your child has **Empathy**

- Your child experiences the day via many feelings. This can be overwhelming, especially for a young person. One of the best things you can do for her is to let her express and sort through her emotions. Just listen to her share the feelings of the day. Give her a safe space to unload, and then move on.

- Your child may need help knowing how to deal with some feelings. Listen and support how she responds to others, and give her suggestions when she is ready.

- Help your child become involved in community activities or school groups that best put her sensitivity and listening talents to use. Whether volunteering in a hospital or nursing home or helping other students with schoolwork, her empathetic ear will be a valuable asset.

- Encourage your child to keep a journal about what she learns when she helps others. These reflections can prepare her to recognize when and how to best use her Empathy talents in the future.

- Understand that your child's need to comfort or assist others isn't because she is a "busybody." Rather, she has an innate need to lend a sensitive ear to friends and family members.

Questions for strengths development

What specific feelings did you notice in another person today?

How can you help your friends, family and coworkers be more aware when someone is troubled or stressed?

When friends come to you to talk, how do you show them that you are trustworthy?

How do you respond when you notice that a friend or another person is having a bad day?

People exceptionally talented

in the Focus theme can take

a direction, follow through

and make the corrections

necessary to stay on track.

They prioritize, then act.

Focus

"Where am I headed?" you ask yourself. You ask this question every day. Guided by this theme of Focus, you need a clear destination. Lacking one, your life and your work can quickly become frustrating. And so each year, each month and even each week you set goals. These goals then serve as your compass, helping you determine priorities and make the necessary corrections to get back on course. Your Focus is powerful because it forces you to filter; you instinctively evaluate whether or not a particular action will help you move toward your goal. Those that don't are ignored. In the end, then, your Focus forces you to be efficient. Naturally, the flip side of this is that it causes you to become impatient with delays, obstacles and even tangents, no matter how intriguing they appear to be. This makes you an extremely valuable team member. When others start to wander down other avenues, you bring them back to the main road. Your Focus reminds everyone that if something is not helping you move toward your destination, then it is not important. And if it is not important, then it is not worth your time. You keep everyone on point.

If you have **Focus**

- Write down your goals. Be sure to include goals that include each of your children every day. Refer to them often, and note the progress you have made toward reaching them. This will give you a sense of advancement and fulfillment every day.

- Give your children mental pictures of who they can be and how they can get there. Find good role models for your children, and arrange for your kids to spend time with them.

- Provide direction for your children and family, whether it is planning a family outing, finishing a home project or working as a team on a task. Name the goal, provide the structure and point them toward the end result.

- Show your children your to-do list. It will help them understand your motivation and may help them decide what to accomplish each day too.

- If your children have short attention spans, use your ability to concentrate and prioritize to keep them on track.

If your child has **Focus**

- Help your child identify people at school or in the community he admires, especially those who have achieved goals he would like to reach. Encourage him to ask them about the steps they took to reach their goals. Talking to role models can help him create and focus on a detailed path to success.

- Encourage your child to write down his daily, weekly, monthly or long-term aspirations. Reinforce activities he chooses that are in line with his objectives.

- Talk to your child regularly about his short-term and long-term goals, both personal and school-related. Celebrate these goals as he achieves them, especially when they are rigorous. And strategize with him about the more difficult ones.

- Ask your child what he has accomplished each day. Ask him what he still has to do.

- Think about how your child can help siblings, friends or other students set goals for themselves. He naturally knows how to stay on track and can help them focus on what they have to accomplish at home or school.

Questions for strengths development

What are your goals right now? Who knows about them? Who can help you reach them?

Where do you see yourself in the future? How do you set timelines and objectives that will help you achieve that vision?

In meetings, classes or group projects, how do you keep everyone on task?

What are you looking forward to accomplishing most today, this week or this weekend? How do you keep track of your progress?

People exceptionally talented

in the Futuristic theme are

inspired by the future and

what could be. They energize

others with their visions of

the future.

Futuristic

Clifton
StrengthsFinder

"Wouldn't it be great if ..." You are the kind of person who loves to peer over the horizon. The future fascinates you. As if it were projected on the wall, you see in detail what the future might hold, and this detailed picture keeps pulling you forward, into tomorrow. While the exact content of the picture will depend on your other strengths and interests — a better product, a better team, a better life or a better world — it will always be inspirational to you. You are a dreamer who sees visions of what could be and who cherishes those visions. When the present proves too frustrating and the people around you too pragmatic, you conjure up your visions of the future and they energize you. They can energize others too. In fact, very often people look to you to describe your visions of the future. They want a picture that can raise their sights and thereby their spirits. You can paint it for them. Practice. Choose your words carefully. Make the picture as vivid as possible. People will want to latch on to the hope you bring.

165

If you have **Futuristic**

- You might see a vision of what your children can be before they do. Describe what you see and talk about your vision with them so they can see it too.

- To many kids, tomorrow often seems far away. When your children can't wait for a big upcoming family event, inspire them with details and paint pictures of what you will see or do. Giving them specific things to focus on might make the time go by faster.

- Share the dreams you had as a young person with your children. While your grown-up life might not exactly match the visions of your youth, talk with your children about how your dreams helped you shape the paths you chose and led to your life today.

- Describe to your children the thoughts, ideas, hopes and dreams you have as your family grows and changes through the years. Talk about activities you envision and why you see them as fun, challenging or beneficial.

- Use your energy for the future as a way to inspire your children when the going gets tough. Remind them what your family's dreams are and how today's activities will move them toward the future.

If your child has **Futuristic**

- Allow your child time to think about the future. Remind her that the more time she spends considering her ideas about the future, the more vivid they will become. The more vivid her ideas, the more persuasive she will be. Encourage her to "dream big."

- Ask your child to write down what she thinks might happen in one year, in five years and in 10 years. Save these ideas and revisit them when each span of time has passed. You will both enjoy seeing how close her predictions were to reality.

- Your child will recognize Futuristic talents in others. Encourage her to develop the Futuristic talents of younger kids by talking with them about their dreams and what they think the future will be like.

- Seek out and connect with teachers who have Futuristic talents. They will appreciate your child's natural talent to think ahead — and like her, they will enjoy talking about what could be.

- Find people your child can talk with about goals and dreams for the future. Forecasting with friends, family and teachers keeps goals and dreams top of mind for her and helps her take action to make them a reality.

Questions for strengths development

Have you shared your visions and plans for the future with anyone?

What difference would you like to make in your community or school? How can you create a future in which you can make that contribution? Who can help you?

What are you putting into action right now that will make the future better for yourself or your family?

What is your ideal job? What do you dream of doing in five years?

People exceptionally talented

in the Harmony theme look

for consensus. They don't

enjoy conflict; rather, they

seek areas of agreement.

Harmony

You look for areas of agreement. In your view there is little to be gained from conflict and friction, so you seek to hold them to a minimum. When you know that the people around you hold differing views, you try to find the common ground. You try to steer them away from confrontation and toward harmony. In fact, harmony is one of your guiding values. You can't quite believe how much time is wasted by people trying to impose their views on others. Wouldn't we all be more productive if we kept our opinions in check and instead looked for consensus and support? You believe we would, and you live by that belief. When others are sounding off about their goals, their claims and their fervently held opinions, you hold your peace. When others strike out in a direction, you will willingly, in the service of harmony, modify your own objectives to merge with theirs (as long as their basic values do not clash with yours). When others start to argue about their pet theory or concept, you steer clear of the debate, preferring to talk about practical, down-to-earth matters on which you can all agree. In your view we are all in the same boat, and we need this boat to get where we are going. It is a good boat. There is no need to rock it just to show that you can.

If you have **Harmony**

- Use your calm and down-to-earth approach to bring stability and practicality to your children, family, workplace and friendships.

- Take a leadership role in your children's activities, groups or clubs. Your Harmony talents can bring people together and smooth the process of working toward a group's collective goals.

- Because you are more comfortable in the middle ground than many people, help your children by being a moderator during times of inevitable conflict. Instead of adding fuel to the fire, help them learn how to create a peaceful and fair resolution.

- When your children are arguing, help them find areas of agreement. Finding a common ground may not totally resolve the issue, but it can be a starting point for working together.

- When you need to make decisions or take action, you believe that collaboration works best. Team up with your partner on parenting decisions. Pull your children into family discussions. You will feel better when you ask questions and gain information and insights from everyone.

If your child has **Harmony**

- Recognize your child for his ability to bring calmness and agreeability to a group. Whether it's with friends or in the classroom, he can use his Harmony talents to help people see where they agree rather than where they disagree and move to solutions more quickly.

- Talk to your child about joining multicultural groups in which he can help people from differing backgrounds come together and appreciate each other. He has the talent to show others that they have more in common than they might first believe.

- Encourage your child to take leadership roles on teams, at school and in community groups. He can help people collaborate to take action that will involve and benefit everyone.

- When beginning a team project or assignment at school, ask your child to clarify the teacher's expectations. This communication will make the task less stressful for everyone because it will help prevent confusion and disagreements.

- Be aware that there might be times when your child needs help saying no — or maybe a reason not to participate. It may be easier for him to say that his parents won't let him do something than to rock the boat by refusing to.

Questions for strengths development

How do you respond to conflict? Do you avoid it or look for ways to make everyone happy?

What groups, clubs or teams do you belong to? How can you help group members share their opinions in a matter-of-fact way?

When people are arguing or in an endless debate, how do you help them find agreement?

How do you keep your focus on practical matters that you can act on?

People exceptionally talented

in the Ideation theme are

fascinated by ideas. They

are able to find connections

between seemingly

disparate phenomena.

Ideation

You are fascinated by ideas. What is an idea? An idea is a concept, the best explanation of the most events. You are delighted when you discover beneath the complex surface an elegantly simple concept to explain why things are the way they are. An idea is a connection. Yours is the kind of mind that is always looking for connections, and so you are intrigued when seemingly disparate phenomena can be linked by an obscure connection. An idea is a new perspective on familiar challenges. You revel in taking the world we all know and turning it around so we can view it from a strange but strangely enlightening angle. You love all these ideas because they are profound, because they are novel, because they are clarifying, because they are contrary, because they are bizarre. For all these reasons you derive a jolt of energy whenever a new idea occurs to you. Others may label you creative or original or conceptual or even smart. Perhaps you are all of these. Who can be sure? What you are sure of is that ideas are thrilling. And on most days this is enough.

If you have **Ideation**

- Use your Ideation talents to help your children come up with creative strategies, whether they need help with a fundraiser, a school project, a slumber party or rearranging their room.

- What do your children find interesting? What do they like to do? Take time to explore and learn more about what they enjoy. Then share your novel perspective to help them clarify, reinforce and see their interests in a new way.

- Collect the ideas you hear from your children. From time to time, revisit and share all the ideas you've gathered with your children and family. They may have forgotten some of them, and reminding them of their ideas might spark interest and action.

- What ideas do you have for family time? Have fun brainstorming with your children and family about activities they want to do and organizations or events they want to get involved with.

- You have the capability to see many perspectives and to consider different viewpoints. Use that capability to broaden your children's outlook by showing them the wide variety of attitudes and opinions in the world.

If your child has **Ideation**

- Help your child choose classes with instructors who involve students in creative projects rather than just exams and term papers. She will appreciate the freedom to apply concepts and will likely promote other students' creativity.

- Partner with your child to take her ideas from concept to actuality. When she has an idea, get her to write it down and list the actions she needs to take to make it happen.

- Trust your child's Ideation talents, and give them a chance to work overtime. When she has good ideas, encourage her to organize and keep them so she can review and develop them later. Even if they don't seem practical or applicable at the time, these ideas may be the start of something big.

- Stimulate and feed your child's Ideation talents by letting her have time to read, surf the Internet or discuss her ideas with others. These activities can provide raw material for new ideas and can help your child refine her thoughts.

- Find classes, clubs or projects that your child can get involved in and use her creative talents. Perhaps writing, photography, graphics, painting or design? These kinds of activities will spur her Ideation talents.

Questions for strengths development

What new concepts are you excited about? Do you have a place where you can go to brainstorm? Have you shared your thoughts with anyone?

When and how do you get your best ideas? What was your best idea today? Did you hear a good idea from anyone else?

How could you use your creativity to help improve your community, neighborhood or school?

Do you record and keep track of your thoughts and the connections you make?

People exceptionally talented

in the Includer theme

accept others. They show

awareness of those who feel

left out and make an effort to

include them.

Includer

"Stretch the circle wider." This is the philosophy around which you orient your life. You want to include people and make them feel part of the group. In direct contrast to those who are drawn only to exclusive groups, you actively avoid those groups that exclude others. You want to expand the group so that as many people as possible can benefit from its support. You hate the sight of someone on the outside looking in. You want to draw them in so that they can feel the warmth of the group. You are an instinctively accepting person. Regardless of race or sex or nationality or personality or faith, you cast few judgments. Judgments can hurt a person's feelings. Why do that if you don't have to? Your accepting nature does not necessarily rest on a belief that each of us is different and that one should respect these differences. Rather, it rests on your conviction that fundamentally we are all the same. We are all equally important. Thus, no one should be ignored. Each of us should be included. It is the least we all deserve.

If you have **Includer**

- Make sure to invite all of your children to all of your family activities. Whether they choose to join or not, being invited makes a difference.

- Be a role model for inclusiveness. Give your children specific examples of people at work or in other settings whom you've included and how it made a positive difference. Explain how groups get work done more effectively when they include a variety of people.

- Challenge your family to be a group where outsiders are welcome. Suggest including friends, neighbors and others in your family's activities. Who would enjoy participating? Who could expand and enrich your family by joining in your activities?

- Explain to your children why you feel being inclusive is important. Young people experience and see rejection on a regular basis. Help them think about the differences "widening the circle" can make.

- Take the initiative in planning group events or social activities. You can be a great connector of people who wouldn't typically get together.

If your child has **Includer**

- Encourage your child to take the lead in welcoming new kids to his school, neighborhood or team. He will be sensitive to newcomers' uneasiness and can help them feel comfortable.

- Ask your child to find opportunities to promote cultural diversity in groups and committees in his school or community. He can make a big difference in fostering awareness and welcoming all kinds of people.

- Connect your child with experienced Includers. Which teachers, students or community leaders do you admire for their ability to involve others? These people can inspire and expand your child's talents to include.

- Keep in mind that your child may need help planning get-togethers or being a part of exclusive clubs or teams because he won't want to leave anyone out. More doesn't always mean better, so he may need help drawing logical conclusions when the list doesn't include everyone.

- Ask your child if he has noticed anyone who is being left out — at school, in peer groups or in the neighborhood — and what he can do to include them. Sometimes he may need to partner with someone who will help him invite others into the circle.

Questions for strengths development

Have you helped anyone feel like part of a group lately? How can you better include people in your daily life and activities?

Have you ever brought people from diverse cultures or backgrounds together? How did that feel?

When you see cliques or exclusive groups at school or work, what can you do to encourage them to become more inclusive?

Do you enjoy speaking up for unheard voices? How can you do that more to make sure everyone is represented?

People exceptionally talented

in the Individualization theme

are intrigued with the unique

qualities of each person.

They have a gift for figuring

out how different people can

work together productively.

Individualization

Clifton StrengthsFinder

Your Individualization theme leads you to be intrigued by the unique qualities of each person. You are impatient with generalizations or "types" because you don't want to obscure what is special and distinct about each person. Instead, you focus on the differences between individuals. You instinctively observe each person's style, each person's motivation, how each thinks and how each builds relationships. You hear the one-of-a-kind stories in each person's life. This theme explains why you pick your friends just the right birthday gift, why you know that one person prefers praise in public and another detests it, and why you tailor your teaching style to accommodate one person's need to be shown and another's desire to "figure it out as I go." Because you are such a keen observer of other people's strengths, you can draw out the best in each person. This Individualization theme also helps you build productive teams. While some search around for the perfect team "structure" or "process," you know instinctively that the secret to great teams is casting by individual strengths so that everyone can do a lot of what they do well.

If you have **Individualization**

- You know what brings out the best in each of your children. Find or create experiences and opportunities for them to shine.

- Help your children appreciate what they each contribute to the family and to the world. Give them examples of what makes each of them unique. Make a point of talking about each child with the entire family.

- Use your Individualization talents when you plan celebrations and parties for your children. Ask them what they like best. A big bash for graduation or a special family dinner? A cake for their birthday or mashed potatoes? They will appreciate the personalized attention.

- Give your children responsibilities based on their individual strengths. Be sure to tell them why you think the responsibility you gave them is a good fit for each of them.

- When planning a family outing, gathering or trip, get everyone's input. Let each family member take a role in the planning based on his or her interests and strengths. It will make the event more fun for everyone.

If your child has **Individualization**

- Suggest to your child that she consider becoming a mentor, tutor or peer counselor. Because she naturally recognizes and respects unique talents and styles, she may be exceptional in these roles.

- Encourage your child to find avenues for her Individualization talents, for example, volunteering for the yearbook or school newspaper and writing about interesting students or teachers. Her observations of others' unique qualities can be entertaining and enlightening.

- Ask your child to study how people who have different ways of looking at life can work together productively — in her school, teams, clubs or community groups and in your family and neighborhood. Tell her that when she uses what she learns to help others see and appreciate their differences, it can have a powerful and positive impact.

- Suggest that your child research people she admires to discover the specific talents that contribute to their success. See if she can notice the similarities and differences between their talents and her own — and that different talents can lead to the same positive outcomes.

- When planning an activity, challenge your child to figure out what would make it the most fun or the most helpful for each participant.

Questions for strengths development

What is unique about your best friend?

How do you identify what others do well, and how do you help them make the most of their individual talents?

Have you ever thought about what you are best at and what makes you unique?

Do you like making your friends and colleagues aware of other people's motivations and explaining their personal styles?

People exceptionally

talented in the Input theme

have a craving to know

more. Often they like to

collect and archive all kinds

of information.

Input

You are inquisitive. You collect things. You might collect information — words, facts, books and quotations — or you might collect tangible objects such as butterflies, baseball cards, porcelain dolls or sepia photographs. Whatever you collect, you collect it because it interests you. And yours is the kind of mind that finds so many things interesting. The world is exciting precisely because of its infinite variety and complexity. If you read a great deal, it is not necessarily to refine your theories but, rather, to add more information to your archives. If you like to travel, it is because each new location offers novel artifacts and facts. These can be acquired and then stored away. Why are they worth storing? At the time of storing it is often hard to say exactly when or why you might need them, but who knows when they might become useful? With all those possible uses in mind, you really don't feel comfortable throwing anything away. So you keep acquiring and compiling and filing stuff away. It's interesting. It keeps your mind fresh. And perhaps one day some of it will prove valuable.

If you have **Input**

- You likely have collected many concrete and practical resources over time. Make sure these valuable collections are available to your children. Tell them about items and knowledge you gathered when you were their age. Highlight what you think is most valuable today or what will be in the future.

- Participate in your children's learning — homework, classes and clubs — by using your natural inquisitiveness to dig up more information. Share what you find with them. This is a great way to build knowledge and shared memories with your children.

- Set up a place to store the things you collect. Make it accessible. Invite everyone in your family to contribute, or let it be a place that inspires your children to ask questions that keep you adding to the collections.

- Use your Input talents to acquire artifacts, objects or information related to your children's areas of interest that can feed their knowledge. Tell your children where and how you found these resources, and talk with them about how they might use them.

- When your children, family or organizations you are involved with face a unique challenge, research all the issues. Share what you find so that, as a group, you can make the best decisions for everyone involved.

If your child has **Input**

- Help your child devise a way to store and easily locate information he has gathered. This can be a simple filing system in his room for magazine articles or a computer database he can maintain.

- Looking for and reading articles or stories online or in the library may seem boring to some people, but your child might enjoy it. He likes to find interesting facts and concepts that he can use in assignments or share with people who will enjoy them. Realize that sometimes he might like collecting information so much that you will need to help him define his parameters.

- Identify opportunities for your child to use his Input talents. Perhaps he can take the lead in gathering information for a group research paper or help a relative who needs information about a health issue.

- Ask your child if he wants to join a debate team, write for the school newspaper or create a blog. His fact-checking abilities can lead to exceptionally solid arguments and articles.

- Talk with your child about how he can use his Input talents to reach goals he has for himself or to help others. For example, when he is working in a group, he could volunteer to gather information on the topic at hand. Or he could be the designated family member who finds information about a place you are going to visit.

Questions for strengths development

What topics do you want to know the most about? How can you learn more about them?

How do you like to learn? Whom do you like to learn from?

What are you reading right now? What is next on your list?

What is one good question you can ask today?

People exceptionally talented

in the Intellection theme

are characterized by their

intellectual activity. They are

introspective and appreciate

intellectual discussions.

Intellection

You like to think. You like mental activity. You like exercising the "muscles" of your brain, stretching them in multiple directions. This need for mental activity may be focused; for example, you may be trying to solve a problem or develop an idea or understand another person's feelings. The exact focus will depend on your other strengths. On the other hand, this mental activity may very well lack focus. The theme of Intellection does not dictate what you are thinking about; it simply describes that you like to think. You are the kind of person who enjoys your time alone because it is your time for musing and reflection. You are introspective. In a sense you are your own best companion, as you pose yourself questions and try out answers on yourself to see how they sound. This introspection may lead you to a slight sense of discontent as you compare what you are actually doing with all the thoughts and ideas that your mind conceives. Or this introspection may tend toward more pragmatic matters such as the events of the day or a conversation that you plan to have later. Wherever it leads you, this mental hum is one of the constants of your life.

If you have **Intellection**

- Be sure to give yourself time and space to be alone and think. It may be early in the morning, at night after the kids are asleep, during your commute to work or while you are exercising. Having this time to think brings wisdom and thoughtfulness to your parenting.

- You think up great questions, and you enjoy asking them. Develop some questions to ask your children about areas where they need help. Use questions to get discussions flowing and to steer them to think about what is in their best interest. Consider coming up with a "question of the week" you could ask everyone in your family.

- Keep track of what you are thinking about and how it could benefit your children. Be sure to share your thoughts with them. Use your musings for dinner conversation or fodder for long car rides.

- Take time to write about your children, your family or your parenting style. Writing or recording your thoughts is a great way to collect and refine them.

- Philosophical and theoretical conversations stimulate your thinking and decision making. Look for others you could engage on a regular basis to discuss child, family and parenting topics.

If your child has **Intellection**

- What is your child most interested in? Challenge her with questions about her interests, and give her problems to solve that will focus her thinking.

- Respect your child's need for time to think. Consider the circumstances in which she does her best thinking. Does she think best alone or with others, in a quiet environment or a noisy one, while in motion or while sitting still? Is there a specific place or time of day? Help her find somewhere at home to ponder, and give her the time she needs.

- Find "big thinkers" — including yourself perhaps — with whom your child can build relationships. She will enjoy the challenge of exchanging ideas with others and may learn methods to refine her own thinking.

- Encourage your child to purposefully schedule time to think and plan before writing a paper or doing an assignment. She will feel more comfortable when she has had some time to muse before jumping in.

- Take time every day to talk with your child about what is on her mind. She may want to talk about her thoughts, ask questions or develop ideas. Listen, but also offer your ideas or questions to stimulate her mental activity.

Questions for strengths development

When is the best time for you to think and work on problems?

What big ideas would you like to think about or discuss?

Which people, classes or activities stimulate your thinking?

What or whom do you find intellectually inspiring?

People exceptionally talented

in the Learner theme have a

great desire to learn and want

to continuously improve.

The process of learning,

rather than the outcome,

excites them.

Learner

You love to learn. The subject matter that interests you most will be determined by your other themes and experiences, but whatever the subject, you will always be drawn to the process of learning. The process, more than the content or the result, is especially exciting for you. You are energized by the steady and deliberate journey from ignorance to competence. The thrill of the first few facts, the early efforts to recite or practice what you have learned, the growing confidence of a skill mastered — this is the process that entices you. Your excitement leads you to engage in adult learning experiences — yoga or piano lessons or graduate classes. It enables you to thrive in dynamic work environments where you are asked to take on short project assignments and are expected to learn a lot about the new subject matter in a short period of time and then move on to the next one. This Learner theme does not necessarily mean that you seek to become the subject matter expert, or that you are striving for the respect that accompanies a professional or academic credential. The outcome of the learning is less significant than the "getting there."

If you have **Learner**

- Study your children. They'll provide you with endless interesting, entertaining and thought-provoking material.

- Use your Learner talents to help you understand what makes your children tick. Learn about stages of development, the process of growth and learning, and the developing mind. This knowledge will help you through the excitement as well as the trials and tribulations of raising children.

- Keep notes or a journal about what you learn. Use your notes as a handy reference for each of your children to help when you or they need to find answers.

- Let your children know how you learn best. They may or may not be as in touch with how they learn as you are. Realize and appreciate that their learning styles may be different from yours.

- Field trips are great learning opportunities. Consider planning field trips to museums, historical landmarks or other educational places for your entire family or for each of your children.

If your child has **Learner**

- Find out how your child learns best. You may only need to ask him. If he learns by teaching, seek out opportunities for him to give presentations. If he learns by doing, look for workshops that teach skills or crafts. He might learn best through silent reflection. If that's the case, set aside some quiet time for him.

- Your child will flourish if he can track his learning progress. If there are distinct levels of achievement within a discipline or skill, be sure to celebrate his progression from level to level. If these levels don't exist, create them — for example, reading five books or making three presentations on a subject.

- Look for clubs or organizations at school or in your community or church that pride themselves on their mission of continually learning. This type of environment will excite your child and challenge his Learner talents. Ask teachers, counselors or fellow students for tips on finding these groups.

- Encourage your child to notice friends who also like to learn. They might enjoy getting together with him for study sessions or field trips involving mutual interests.

- Suggest to your child that he keep notes or a journal about things he learned in a favorite class or group. This can be a great way to save valuable information and lessons he can use later.

Questions for strengths development

Of your current classes, activities or projects, what are you most excited about?

How do you learn best — by doing, teaching, reading, experimenting, thinking alone, or discussing and brainstorming with others?

What specific topics would you like to learn more about? How can you become an expert at them?

What one new thing did you learn today? What do you want to learn this week?

People exceptionally talented

in the Maximizer theme focus

on strengths as a way to

stimulate personal and group

excellence. They seek to

transform something strong

into something superb.

Maximizer

Excellence, not average, is your measure. Taking something from below average to slightly above average takes a great deal of effort and in your opinion is not very rewarding. Transforming something strong into something superb takes just as much effort but is much more thrilling. Strengths, whether yours or someone else's, fascinate you. Like a diver after pearls, you search them out, watching for the telltale signs of a strength. A glimpse of untutored excellence, rapid learning, a skill mastered without recourse to steps — all these are clues that a strength may be in play. And having found a strength, you feel compelled to nurture it, refine it and stretch it toward excellence. You polish the pearl until it shines. This natural sorting of strengths means that others see you as discriminating. You choose to spend time with people who appreciate your particular strengths. Likewise, you are attracted to others who seem to have found and cultivated their own strengths. You tend to avoid those who want to fix you and make you well-rounded. You don't want to spend your life bemoaning what you lack. Rather, you want to capitalize on the gifts with which you are blessed. It's more fun. It's more productive. And, counterintuitively, it is more demanding.

If you have **Maximizer**

- Use your discriminating nature to identify the best things about each of your children.

- As you naturally seek excellence, remember that your children may not meet the standards you have set as an adult. Highlight their strong points and notice what they are good at before telling them how to improve. Build on what they are already doing well to increase their confidence and keep them moving forward.

- Find teachers, coaches, neighbors or counselors who can build relationships that make the most of your children's unique talents. Look for those who are most likely to appreciate your children's particular strengths.

- Be a model for your children by telling each of them what he or she does best. Do the same for their friends, your friends, your family and other people in your life.

- Study successful people, past and present. Spend time with people who have developed their talents into strengths. The more you understand how strengths lead to success, the more likely you will be to create success in your children's lives.

If your child has **Maximizer**

- Encourage your child to tell her friends and family what they're doing well. Most people find it difficult to describe or even recognize what they do best, so they will appreciate and gain confidence from her observations.

- Your child maximizes others, so be sure to find mentors who will maximize her. Because she naturally focuses on other people, she may be distracted from her own strengths. Make sure she has frequent contact with people who will challenge her and keep her pointed toward excellence.

- Help your child find groups, clubs or teams to join that do great work and have high levels of performance. Belonging to a group where members "just show up" won't be a good experience for her because she needs to be part of something excellent that matters to her.

- Talk with your child about how she can help friends, siblings or other family members excel. Perhaps she could describe to them what they're doing well before telling them how they can improve. Focusing on other people's talents will build their confidence and will allow your child to put her talents into action.

- As a Maximizer, excellence is the standard for your child. Understand that sometimes, you may need to help her decide when to keep going and when to move on.

Questions for strengths development

What part of your life could be better? How can you make it better? What is good but could be great?

How do you feel when you have to solve problems or fix something that is broken? Could you find a partner to help you troubleshoot?

Have you ever pointed out what your friends and family members are great at? How can you help them see and understand their own strengths?

What can you do to refine your talents and skills? How can you measure your own progress toward excellence?

People exceptionally talented

in the Positivity theme have

contagious enthusiasm.

They are upbeat and can get

others excited about what

they are going to do.

Positivity

You are generous with praise, quick to smile and always on the lookout for the positive in the situation. Some call you lighthearted. Others just wish that their glass were as full as yours seems to be. But either way, people want to be around you. Their world looks better around you because your enthusiasm is contagious. Lacking your energy and optimism, some find their world drab with repetition or, worse, heavy with pressure. You seem to find a way to lighten their spirit. You inject drama into every project. You celebrate every achievement. You find ways to make everything more exciting and more vital. Some cynics may reject your energy, but you are rarely dragged down. Your Positivity won't allow it. Somehow you can't quite escape your conviction that it is good to be alive, that work can be fun and that no matter what the setbacks, one must never lose one's sense of humor.

If you have **Positivity**

- Your positive temperament is great to be around. Make your kids laugh every day. It will keep them coming back to you when their joy and optimism fade.

- Use your Positivity talents to help your children and family whether times are good or bad. Your consistently positive perspective can help others maintain focus and hope.

- When your children, family and others find it difficult to stay positive, help them see the bright side of a situation or the good in other people.

- Plan celebrations for your children, your family, your community and your children's school. No matter what you're celebrating, you have the ability to make events and activities fun and memorable.

- Explain to your children how focusing on the best aspects of a situation or a person can create better outcomes. Give them specific examples to show them the value of positivity.

If your child has **Positivity**

- Remind your child that he can make learning fun for others. Talk to his teachers, and share your ideas about how he can naturally energize and stimulate classmates with his praise and excitement.

- Your child can express his Positivity talents in many ways. Help him notice when other people need hope and encouragement, and inspire him to use his natural optimism to cheer them up.

- Consider having your child help plan family, school or community celebrations. He has the ability to turn small achievements into memorable events, and people are likely to look forward to the recognition.

- Ask teachers and sponsors to identify projects or groups that would benefit from your child's Positivity talents. His enthusiastic spirit can help others meet challenges, reach goals and have a lot of fun along the way.

- The positive energy your child brings to any group can give everyone perspective and hope. Remind him that his optimistic attitude and enthusiasm can make a real difference.

Questions for strengths development

How have you helped your friends or family have fun lately?

How do you feel when you are faced with a challenge? How do you manage those feelings?

Do others notice your optimistic outlook on life?

When was the last time you made another person smile or laugh?

People exceptionally talented

in the Relator theme enjoy

close relationships with

others. They find deep

satisfaction in working hard

with friends to achieve a goal.

Relator

Clifton
StrengthsFinder

Relator describes your attitude toward your relationships. In simple terms, the Relator theme pulls you toward people you already know. You do not necessarily shy away from meeting new people — in fact, you may have other themes that cause you to enjoy the thrill of turning strangers into friends — but you do derive a great deal of pleasure and strength from being around your close friends. You are comfortable with intimacy. Once the initial connection has been made, you deliberately encourage a deepening of the relationship. You want to understand their feelings, their goals, their fears and their dreams; and you want them to understand yours. You know that this kind of closeness implies a certain amount of risk — you might be taken advantage of — but you are willing to accept that risk. For you a relationship has value only if it is genuine. And the only way to know that is to entrust yourself to the other person. The more you share with each other, the more you risk together. The more you risk together, the more each of you proves your caring is genuine. These are your steps toward real friendship, and you take them willingly.

If you have **Relator**

- Schedule regular one-on-one time with each of your children. Your undivided attention will strengthen your relationship with them.

- You naturally form deep friendships. Use the trust you have built to create effective partnerships. Team up with another parent who is a good friend to make positive changes in your children's lives — for example, safer streets or more opportunities for exercise.

- Consider taking a family vacation with your children's close friends and their families. Some people would be uncomfortable spending a lot of time with another family, but you might find that it satisfies your Relator talents.

- You need time to talk deeply and meaningfully. Make sure you get that opportunity. Long car rides and midnight-snack meet-ups can stimulate great conversations with your children.

- The relationships you build can help your children in many ways. Consider connecting with your children's friends' parents to build community and understanding. Create a positive platform to work from in good times and bad.

If your child has **Relator**

- Suggest that your child form study groups with close friends. When she can talk about class material with her good friends, she will understand it better.

- Tell your child that she can be an important role model for trust. When she shows people who are close to her that she trusts them, they may be more likely to become trusting, and trustworthy, themselves.

- Tell your child that no matter how busy she is, she should stay in contact with her best friends. They are her fuel.

- Find counselors, fellow students and favorite past teachers who can help your child select new teachers who will take the time to get to know her as a person. She will have better experiences in class when the teacher takes an interest in her.

- When someone lets your child down, she will take it seriously and might become nervous about remaining friends with that person. To prevent her from giving up on an important relationship, ask her to consider the circumstances — and to be willing to extend trust again if it is deserved.

Questions for strengths development

Which friends or coworkers do you like to spend most of your time with? What do you like best about each one?

How do you learn more about the people you meet? Do you share details about yourself to deepen a new relationship?

What does being a friend mean to you?

How do you show the important people in your life how much you care about them? What can you do to strengthen your closest relationships?

People exceptionally talented

in the Responsibility theme

take psychological ownership

of what they say they will

do. They are committed to

stable values such as honesty

and loyalty.

Responsibility

Your Responsibility theme forces you to take psychological ownership for anything you commit to, and whether large or small, you feel emotionally bound to follow it through to completion. Your good name depends on it. If for some reason you cannot deliver, you automatically start to look for ways to make it up to the other person. Apologies are not enough. Excuses and rationalizations are totally unacceptable. You will not quite be able to live with yourself until you have made restitution. This conscientiousness, this near obsession for doing things right, and your impeccable ethics, combine to create your reputation: utterly dependable. When assigning new responsibilities, people will look to you first because they know it will get done. When people come to you for help — and they soon will — you must be selective. Your willingness to volunteer may sometimes lead you to take on more than you should.

If you have **Responsibility**

- You are driven by your commitments. Talk with your children about the promises you make and the responsibility you feel. Tell them what you are committed to and why it is important to you.

- Sometimes you will have to say no to your kids because of work. Make sure there are also times when you say no to your work because of your kids.

- When you are wrapped up in work or other activities, explain to your children and family why. Tell them why you feel responsible. Use your natural conscientiousness to be a role model for being dependable and reliable.

- Responsibility comes from psychological ownership. Be aware that just telling your children what to do is not as powerful as giving them meaningful choices.

- Many schools, clubs, teams and other groups need reliable parents to take charge. Find groups with projects that are important to you and your children. By contributing your Responsibility talents, you can ensure that these groups meet important goals.

If your child has **Responsibility**

- Give your child responsibilities that are appropriate for his age and ability. Make sure to give him duties that are significant to him and that will feel like true responsibility.

- Your child works best when he has the independence and freedom to follow through on his commitments. Let him know that you don't need to check in while he is working on a project — just at the end.

- You can trust your child to get things done. At the same time, remember that if he has a lot going on, you may need to help him with time management.

- Encourage your child to keep a checklist of things to do and to check off each item as he completes it. To-do lists are both motivating and satisfying for him.

- Be aware that your child may be more responsible than his age might suggest. He thrives on meeting commitments, and his talents might lead him to be conscientious beyond his years.

Questions for strengths development

What do you feel responsible for right now?

Do you ever feel guilty? For what, and when?

Would you like more responsibility at school, home or work? How can you get it?

How does it feel when you deliver on your commitments and promises to others?

People exceptionally talented

in the Restorative theme

are adept at dealing with

problems. They are good at

figuring out what is wrong

and resolving it.

Restorative

You love to solve problems. Whereas some are dismayed when they encounter yet another breakdown, you can be energized by it. You enjoy the challenge of analyzing the symptoms, identifying what is wrong and finding the solution. You may prefer practical problems or conceptual ones or personal ones. You may seek out specific kinds of problems that you have met many times before and that you are confident you can fix. Or you may feel the greatest push when faced with complex and unfamiliar problems. Your exact preferences are determined by your other themes and experiences. But what is certain is that you enjoy bringing things back to life. It is a wonderful feeling to identify the undermining factor(s), eradicate them and restore something to its true glory. Intuitively, you know that without your intervention, this thing — this machine, this technique, this person, this company — might have ceased to function. You fixed it, resuscitated it, rekindled its vitality. Phrasing it the way you might, you saved it.

If you have **Restorative**

- Show your children that problems are a normal part of life and that most can be solved. When you focus on solutions, it helps your children see pathways for dealing with difficulties.

- Be the parent who fixes problems. Remember that while you lead with this theme, others may not. Remember too, children are developing, and some problems do not have an immediate fix. Think about how you could break solutions into steps to help your children understand your process.

- Make sure your children know that you like to solve tricky issues. When they understand that, they might be more willing to share because they know you want to help, whether they have a broken bicycle, computer problem or trouble with a friend.

- While you are drawn toward solving problems, remember that in the long run, it is beneficial to teach your children how to solve problems themselves. Before you rush to fix everything, work with your children to solve problems together.

- Hearing bad news can be hard for many people, especially children. When you hear unpleasant news, you quickly focus on solutions. Use this approach to help your children productively find their way through adverse circumstances toward clarity.

If your child has **Restorative**

- Encourage your child to tell her friends that she enjoys solving problems. They will be more likely to share difficulties when they understand that she is glad to help and likes looking for solutions.

- Your child might get a lot out of a group or club that deals with solving problems or restoring something to its original condition. She can meet challenges that others might find difficult, and she will enjoy making the unworkable workable.

- Talk with your child about how she can use her Restorative talents to serve the community. Together, make a list of ways she can help, such as volunteering to restore blighted areas in your neighborhood or fundraising for causes that are important to her.

- Help your child think about occupations that might be the best fit for her. Home renovators, healthcare providers, mechanics, IT workers and gardeners all restore people, things or processes. Steer her to an internship at an appropriate organization if she is older. For a younger child, take a family field trip to a company that fixes problems.

- Encourage your child to think of any task or activity as a way to improve herself. What obstacles will she need to overcome? What problems will she need to solve? Working on self-improvement can motivate her, especially as she conquers challenges along the way.

Questions for strengths development

What is something you have fixed or made better recently? What problems have you solved? How did you solve them?

Do your friends, family and coworkers know that you like to fix things and work on problems? Could you make their lives easier by telling them?

Have you ever restored or revitalized something that was broken or failing? Have you ever turned a bad situation around?

If you could change one thing for the better, what would it be and how would you change it?

People exceptionally talented

in the Self-Assurance

theme feel confident in

their ability to manage their

own lives. They possess an

inner compass that gives

them confidence that their

decisions are right.

Self-Assurance

Clifton
StrengthsFinder

Self-Assurance is similar to self-confidence. In the deepest part of you, you have faith in your strengths. You know that you are able — able to take risks, able to meet new challenges, able to stake claims and, most important, able to deliver. But Self-Assurance is more than just self-confidence. Blessed with the theme of Self-Assurance, you have confidence not only in your abilities but in your judgment. When you look at the world, you know that your perspective is unique and distinct. And because no one sees exactly what you see, you know that no one can make your decisions for you. No one can tell you what to think. They can guide. They can suggest. But you alone have the authority to form conclusions, make decisions and act. This authority, this final accountability for the living of your life, does not intimidate you. On the contrary, it feels natural to you. No matter what the situation, you seem to know what the right decision is. This theme lends you an aura of certainty. Unlike many, you are not easily swayed by someone else's arguments, no matter how persuasive they may be. This Self-Assurance may be quiet or loud, depending on your other themes, but it is solid. It is strong. Like the keel of a ship, it withstands many different pressures and keeps you on your course.

217

CLIFTON STRENGTHSFINDER — SELF-ASSURANCE

If you have **Self-Assurance**

- Parenting involves its share of disappointments and crises. Rely on your capacity to bounce back fast from setbacks, and use it to help other parents who might not be as confident or certain.

- Build a strong base with your children and family to give you confidence in what matters most to you. You know that investing in your children will pay off, and you know the right plan for them. Because of your relationship, your kids trust you and will listen and act on your advice. Take energy from that.

- While you have confidence in your parenting decisions, think about other people you could talk to whose opinions and perspective would be valuable for you to hear. Listen to what they have to say to support or reconsider your own decisions.

- Your Self-Assurance talents can give your children a sense of security, especially during challenging times. Use your confidence to give them courage and to show them the path and direction you believe will be most helpful.

- Help your children make decisions. They may not have the same confidence you do, so encourage and support them as they navigate their course to make choices.

If your child has **Self-Assurance**

- Help your child choose classes and school groups that he will find challenging and intriguing. His Self-Assurance talents can help him persist and succeed in situations that might intimidate others.

- Remind your child that his self-confidence can inspire other students, friends and siblings who feel shy or nervous. He can be a role model and provide the spark others need to become part of the action.

- Help your child understand that to build trust with others who might not understand his Self-Assurance talents, he needs to give them solid reasons for being trustworthy. His rationale and confidence will resonate with others, giving them confidence in him as well.

- Advise your child to get to know his teachers. Knowing who his teachers are and what they expect will help him feel in control of his learning and give him added confidence.

- Steer your child toward leadership positions in groups that deal with matters that are important to him. Combining his Self-Assurance talents with his personal mission can make a big difference at school or in your community.

Questions for strengths development

How does your intuition guide you? What are you sure you can do?

Do you like to persuade others to see your point of view?

What risks have you taken recently? What is your confidence level when you take risks?

Do friends, coworkers or family members often rely on you to make decisions?

People exceptionally talented

in the Significance theme

want to be very important

in others' eyes. They are

independent and want to

be recognized.

Significance

You want to be very significant in the eyes of other people. In the truest sense of the word you want to be recognized. You want to be heard. You want to stand out. You want to be known. In particular, you want to be known and appreciated for the unique strengths you bring. You feel a need to be admired as credible, professional and successful. Likewise, you want to associate with others who are credible, professional and successful. And if they aren't, you will push them to achieve until they are. Or you will move on. An independent spirit, you want your work to be a way of life rather than a job, and in that work you want to be given free rein, the leeway to do things your way. Your yearnings feel intense to you, and you honor those yearnings. And so your life is filled with goals, achievements or qualifications that you crave. Whatever your focus — and each person is distinct — your Significance theme will keep pulling you upward, away from the mediocre toward the exceptional. It is the theme that keeps you reaching.

If you have **Significance**

- Realize that your desire to be seen as a great parent is a powerful motivator that will ultimately benefit your children.

- Who do you want to be in your children's eyes? What are the most important ways for you to be heard, especially as a parent? Strive to be the best parent you can be through what you say and do each day.

- Fifty years from now, how will you be remembered, and what will your legacy be? Write down the answers to those questions now and begin consciously working toward achieving those goals with your children and family.

- Your Significance talents propel you and put you in the forefront. Explain to your children why you think being seen and heard matters and how it can help define your family.

- What makes you most proud of each of your children and of your family as a whole? Tell them. Talk about it at family meetings or at the dinner table. They will appreciate the positive recognition and attention, and you will feed your Significance talents through your association with them.

If your child has **Significance**

- Ask your child about her best moment of recognition or praise. What was it for? Who gave it? Who was the audience? The answers to these questions can help you re-create more moments like that for her. Help her find classes, clubs or projects that will increase her chances for recognition. She will thrive on the attention.

- Your child's reputation is important to her, even in the smallest details. List the goals, achievements and qualifications she would like to be known for, and help her determine the steps to get there. Ask her to describe individuals she looks up to, whether peers or adults. What do these admirable people do to create their reputations?

- Ask your child what she can do in her school or community that will help her stand out or become well-known. Suggest activities like running for student council, taking a leadership position in an extracurricular club, giving public speeches or volunteering to direct a community service project.

- Look for classes that offer individual recognition for completing challenging independent assignments. Your child will find these classes highly motivating and rewarding.

- Have your child write down the words that best describe her, and tell her to refer to the list frequently. Top-of-mind awareness of her talents will help her maintain the confidence she needs if her "audience" does not respond as positively as expected.

Questions for strengths development

What achievements do you want credit and recognition for? What type of recognition do you prefer?

Whom do you want to receive recognition from?

Where or when have you shown how significant your contributions can be?

Do you ever leave an activity knowing you made a difference? How do you know?

People exceptionally talented

in the Strategic theme create

alternative ways to proceed.

Faced with any given

scenario, they can quickly

spot the relevant patterns

and issues.

Strategic

The Strategic theme enables you to sort through the clutter and find the best route. It is not a skill that can be taught. It is a distinct way of thinking, a special perspective on the world at large. This perspective allows you to see patterns where others simply see complexity. Mindful of these patterns, you play out alternative scenarios, always asking, "What if this happened? Okay, well what if this happened?" This recurring question helps you see around the next corner. There you can evaluate accurately the potential obstacles. Guided by where you see each path leading, you start to make selections. You discard the paths that lead nowhere. You discard the paths that lead straight into resistance. You discard the paths that lead into a fog of confusion. You cull and make selections until you arrive at the chosen path — your strategy. Armed with your strategy, you strike forward. This is your Strategic theme at work: "What if?" Select. Strike.

If you have **Strategic**

- Use your talent to see and consider multiple options to guide your children when they don't know what to do next. Your ability to objectively talk through "what if" scenarios can be very helpful to your children, regardless of their age.

- When you see your children working toward a goal and have an idea, tell them the steps you think they should take to attain the goal. You have a natural ability to see the best path.

- Let your children know that you like to think through many options for reaching a goal. Tell them about times when you have done this in your life, especially when you were their age.

- Others, including your children, might not always see the value of strategic thinking as clearly as you do. So be prepared to explain your plan to them and why you believe it will lead to the best outcome. Learn how to describe what you see down the road.

- How can you optimize your time with your children and your family? Ask yourself "what if" questions: What if I spent less time ___ and more time ___? Think about how the different scenarios you come up with could make a difference to your children and family.

If your child has **Strategic**

- Partner your child with exceptional Activators and Achievers. While he can see the best path, others can make sure he gets going and arrives at the destination.

- When your child has a goal in mind, he will sort through the ways he can reach that goal. Help him gather as much information as possible as he considers the best options.

- Let your child's teachers know that he thrives when he is engaged in conversations about alternatives for different situations or about problem solving to get an assignment done. Detailed discussions like this can challenge and sharpen his strategic thinking.

- Trust your child's Strategic talent. Although you might sometimes have difficulty understanding this talent or his choices, his brain is naturally suited to tactical thinking. Encourage him to have confidence in his plans and to share them with others.

- Help your child join a group that you both think does important work. What are some real-world issues or needs that your child could strategize about with others? His strategic thinking talents can be a powerful force for a good cause.

Questions for strengths development

What is a goal you achieved recently? How did you choose the route you took to achieve that goal?

When others see only the pieces, how do you help them see the big picture?

Have you ever helped a friend or coworker make a decision? How did you help?

How do you apply your natural "what if" thinking to what you need to accomplish today? This week? This year?

People exceptionally talented

in the Woo theme love the

challenge of meeting new

people and winning them

over. They derive satisfaction

from breaking the ice

and making a connection

with someone.

Woo

Woo stands for winning others over. You enjoy the challenge of meeting new people and getting them to like you. Strangers are rarely intimidating to you. On the contrary, strangers can be energizing. You are drawn to them. You want to learn their names, ask them questions and find some area of common interest so that you can strike up a conversation and build rapport. Some people shy away from starting up conversations because they worry about running out of things to say. You don't. Not only are you rarely at a loss for words; you actually enjoy initiating with strangers because you derive satisfaction from breaking the ice and making a connection. Once that connection is made, you are quite happy to wrap it up and move on. There are new people to meet, new rooms to work, new crowds to mingle in. In your world there are no strangers, only friends you haven't met yet — lots of them.

If you have **Woo**

- Introduce some of the many people you know to your children. It can be fun for them to get to know a variety of individuals. Meeting new people might encourage your kids to get started on building their own networks.

- Try to get to know the names of all the people in your children's lives. You easily make initial connections that can lead to mutually positive and beneficial relationships for your children.

- Social initiative comes easily to you. Use your Woo talents to bring people together — other families, neighbors, clubs or teams. Connect others who will help support your children and family.

- Your ability to interact and relate to people can help your children and others — especially those who are shy — feel included and part of the group. You create fun and draw people in. Make the most of this natural ability to help your children's friends enjoy spending time at your home.

- You initiate conversations and create connections that serve your children well. Who are some other parents, coaches, neighbors or kids you can talk to? Capitalize on your social talents to put everyone at ease during the first day of school orientation, at a neighborhood picnic or when starting a new role.

If your child has **Woo**

- Ask your child to think about joining groups at school or in the community that need people to meet and greet newcomers and visitors. She can help people get connected right away.

- Let your child schedule time to study and read with others. This interpersonal interaction will stimulate her learning process.

- People with Woo are natural campaigners. Encourage your child to campaign for people and causes that match her values.

- Recognize that the ability to get people to like you is valuable. Help your child understand that, and urge her not to be afraid to use her talents to win others over.

- Let your child know that in social situations, she can help those who are not as outgoing feel more comfortable.

Questions for strengths development

Have you met a new student, neighbor or coworker recently? How did you break the ice?

Would you rather spend time with people you already know or with new friends? Why?

How do you engage people in conversations?

How do others react when you meet and greet people at social functions?

Achieving   Discoverer
Caring   Future Thinker
Competing   Organizer
Confidence   Presence
Dependability   Relating

Clifton Youth StrengthsExplorer

From a rich history of more than 50 years of research and thousands of studies on individuals' talents, Gallup created the Clifton Youth StrengthsExplorer assessment to help children 10-14 years old discover and develop the unique talents within them.

The assessment can help you:

- identify and learn more about your child's unique talents
- help your child apply his natural patterns of thought, feeling and behavior to activities he is involved in
- influence your child's achievement
- better match your child to developmental experiences that foster growth

This assessment is unlike any other test your child has taken in many ways. The most important difference is that while many tests focus on what children don't know or can't do, the Clifton Youth StrengthsExplorer shines a light on your child's potential strengths with a language designed to affirm and encourage his development. The assessment identifies 10 themes of talent — areas where your child's greatest potential for building strengths exists.

Each Clifton Youth StrengthsExplorer talent theme is a filter. A child with a great sense of humor will seize a moment to tell a joke. A child with a strong desire to learn may get on the Internet, even after a project is finished, to find out more about the topic. A child who naturally connects with others will take the initiative to meet the new kid in school even if his close friends don't. A child who is competitive will naturally be emotional about losing. A child who loves to organize may rearrange her room more often than her parents think is necessary. Through the themes filter, these behaviors are examples of talent in the Presence, Discoverer, Relating, Competing and Organizer themes.

The Clifton Youth StrengthsExplorer report will help you better understand your child's filters. You can also use it to recognize how different his filters may be from your own and from those of other children, relatives and peers. The age span of 10-14 includes a tremendous range of development, behavior, maturity and thinking. Children's perceptions of the world are naturally different from those of adults.

TAKING THE ASSESSMENT

Recommended age level:
Children aged 10-14

This book includes an access code that your child can use to take the Clifton Youth StrengthsExplorer assessment. This unique code is in the packet in the back of the book. The online assessment takes about 15-20 minutes to complete. Once it is completed, your child will receive a report that contains an in-depth description of his top three themes of talent. His report will be specifically about his unique talents and includes a guide for your child as well as one for you with suggestions to consider as you help your child develop his talents into strengths.

As you examine your child's top three talent themes in greater detail, read this section for each theme's definition; action items for your child; action items for you; words that describe the theme; questions you can ask your child; and theme contrasts, which highlight the similarities and differences between themes using comparison.

You have more energy

and more goals than other

people. You love a sense

of accomplishment.

Achieving

You have more energy and more goals than other people. You love a sense of accomplishment.

You are in a hurry to get started and make things happen because you almost always have a list in your mind of the things you want to get done. It is fun to achieve small goals and even more exciting to achieve big goals that challenge you. The more you get done, the more you feel like a successful person. And the more successes you have, the more you want to have. Finishing a project feels good to you because you love a sense of accomplishment. An award, a good grade or praise can mean a lot to you because it feels good when your effort and ability are noticed. Because you are a hard worker, you always feel that you could and should be doing more.

Action items for children with **Achieving**

- People might tell you that you are a "self-starter" because you are always working on something. Think about all the things you want to do. Make a list, and decide what is most important. Then, do those things first.

- Challenges are important to you. If every goal on your list is easy, it might not feel good. Set some big goals. Do you want to learn another language, score three goals in a game, write a song or teach yourself to skateboard? Set some goals that will really make you feel proud when you accomplish them.

- You're at your best when you are active and energetic. Find activities that get you up and moving. Are there new things you can do to use your energy to achieve a goal? For example, could you get up early to play your guitar, read, exercise or do your homework?

- You can work harder and longer than most people. Try to be an example and motivate people who are working together on teams or big projects. Sometimes, just one very hard worker helps the whole group get more done.

- What groups could you join to help them accomplish their goals? Think about joining a volunteer group in your church or school. That might be a great place to use your hardworking talents toward important results.

Action items for parents of children with **Achieving**

- Achieving children have more energy than other kids. Think about how your child likes to channel her energy. Are there any activities, projects or responsibilities you could suggest that align with her interests?

- At the end of each day, help your child realize what she accomplished. Ask her what she achieved that day. Then listen to, appreciate and recognize her successes. Point out everything you noticed as well.

- How can you best showcase your child's accomplishments? Find ways to display what she has done. You could create a wall of photos; a scrapbook; a portfolio; a refrigerator display; or a list of daily, weekly or monthly achievements.

Words that describe this theme

self-starter	independent	intense
worker	finisher	self-motivated
producer	driven	productive
doer	diligent	ambitious

Questions for your child

What was your favorite accomplishment this week?

How did you use your energy today to achieve a goal?

What is the best compliment you have received recently, and what was it for?

What challenging goal is on your mind?

Theme contrasts

Achieving: You want to get it done.
Competing: You want to win.

Achieving: You will do what you need to do.
Dependability: You will do what you say you'll do.

In your heart, helping other

people is very important.

You want to make the world

better by helping people in

small ways or big ways.

Caring

In your heart, helping other people is very important. You want to make the world better by helping people in small ways or big ways.

You have a big heart. You feel good when you reach out and help people. You are the friend who includes others. When someone feels left out, you help him or her be part of your group. It is easy for you to encourage people, share with them and help them learn. You know you have something to offer other people. Even the smallest kind deed is important in people's everyday lives. Whether you help in big or small ways, you can make a difference in your world. People count on you to be kind, thoughtful and caring.

Action items for children with **Caring**

- How can you help someone you know? Choose one thing and start doing it this week. Here are some ideas:
    - babysit
    - visit a neighbor
    - do homework with a friend
    - wash dishes for your family
    - mow the lawn or shovel snow for an elderly person
    - collect cans for recycling
    - welcome a new kid at school
    - straighten up the classroom for your teacher
    - walk your neighbor's dog

- When you notice that someone has been left out, invite that person to play, study or sit at your lunch table with you and your friends. You can help people feel welcome, included and happy.

- Can you help someone with schoolwork after yours is done? By sharing what you know, you can help others learn. Take time to tell them "good job" when they do well. You'll both feel good.

- Younger kids may look to you as a friend. Think of ways to teach them new things or how to make them smile. They need bigger kids like you to care about them and show them why they are special.

- How do you show your family that you care about them? Let your family members know that you like being with them. Think about ways you can spend more time together, like playing games or riding bikes. Get their ideas about what is fun to do as a group. Thank them for the best times you have together.

Action items for parents of children with **Caring**

- "Catch" your child being helpful, and respect the power of caring. Acknowledge and affirm his considerate actions. Tell him how his Caring talents make the world a better place for everyone.

- Talk with your Caring child about how helping is part of your own daily life. Share formal and informal ways you help in the workplace, home, school or community. These conversations will spark his thinking about everyday ways to help.

- What are some classroom, school, community or church projects that could use your child's Caring talents? Consider how you could facilitate opportunities for him to lend a hand. Brainstorm with him about these opportunities, which might include:

  - tutoring another student or being a kindergarten buddy

  - helping coach a younger sports team

  - cleaning up a neighborhood park

  - volunteering at an animal shelter or nursing home

  - taking part in a clothing or canned food drive

  - raising funds for an international aid project

Words that describe this theme

big-hearted	cheerleader	friendly
includer	nurturer	thoughtful
devoted	volunteer	kind

Questions for your child

What are three of your favorite ways to help people?

How do you show your family that you care about them?

How can you encourage other students in your classes?

How could you be of assistance in school, community or church projects?

Theme contrasts

Caring: Helping people is important to you.
Relating: Relationships are important to you.

Caring: Others trust that you will make them feel better.
Dependability: Others trust that you will follow through.

You see many things in life as

a game, and you feel great

joy when you win. You truly

hate to lose because you are

always striving for first place.

Competing

You see many things in life as a game, and you feel great joy when you win. You truly hate to lose because you are always striving for first place.

Every day you compete. Winning first place is your goal in any contest that you feel is worth your time. If there is no one to compete against, you compete against yourself to do more or accomplish a goal faster or better. You can be competing against someone else even when that person doesn't know it. Because you hate to lose, you might get angry, upset or even cry. It does not matter if others think the contest is important. If you are doing it, you want to be number one. Others look to you for the motivation to win.

Action items for children with **Competing**

- Winning is a good motivator. Use your built-in need to win at home, at school and in other activities. If you play sports, practice your skills over and over so you are prepared to win. For schoolwork, try to make studying into a game you can win. If your club is having a fundraiser, suggest a contest to see who can raise the most money.

- Other people may give up when they don't see a way to win, but you keep thinking. Try different ways to win, and look for the easiest and fastest way. Maybe there is a shortcut that gets you to your goal sooner.

- Think of ways to measure whatever you are doing. Working on your basketball shot? Keep track of how many baskets you can make in a row. Learning to play a song? Count how many measures you can play without making a mistake. You will find that measurement improves your performance.

- Competing with someone else can help you get better. Do you have other competitive friends you could challenge? Do you have a friend who is as good as or better than you at something? Have a contest with one of these friends. Your friendly competition will push each of you to be better and to do your best.

- Tell a parent, teacher, sister or brother about one thing you really want to do this week. Have this person help you set a challenge for yourself. Can you learn your spelling words in two days? Can you dribble a soccer ball 35 times? Can you learn the names of five new people? Being accountable to someone else will motivate you to meet the challenge.

Action items for parents of children with **Competing**

- Your Competing child may express strong emotions, win or lose. Affirm her feelings — happy or mad — by listening. You may need to help her work through them. Understand that these emotions give your child fuel.

- Help your child measure her progress or success. Make note of her best performance, score or achievement to date. Track big accomplishments or everyday activities, like the most minutes she practices the clarinet or the most pages she reads in a week.

- There are many different ways to compete. Determine what arena suits your child best — sports, arts, academia or clubs. Is she a team or individual competitor? Arrange for her to compete against others to help her stretch her skills.

Words that describe this theme

winner	measurer	self-comparison
scorekeeper	champion	aspiring
comparer	top performer	results-oriented

Questions for your child

What did you do more of or better than someone else this week?

What is one thing you really want to get better at? What challenge can you set for yourself?

Do you have a friend who is as good as or better than you at something? How can you challenge each other in a way that will make you both better?

Which class could you raise your grades in? How can you make studying into a game you can win?

Theme contrasts

Competing: When you watch others perform, you get better.
Presence: When others watch you perform, you get better.

Competing: Winning is the goal.
Achieving: Accomplishing your goal is the goal.

You believe in yourself and

what you can do. This helps

you take on challenges

because you feel sure you

can succeed.

Confidence

You believe in yourself and what you can do. This helps you take on challenges because you feel sure you can succeed.

Because you are confident, you are able to do things that others may not want to try. Knowing that you are a unique and special person in the world gives you the power to be who you are. You don't have to be like everybody else, and you don't have to follow the crowd. Even when you don't feel it, other people may see you as brave because you will speak up even if no one else will. You are sure enough of your opinions that you will take a stand for them. It is great to believe in what you can do because this belief helps you do more in your life.

Action items for children with **Confidence**

- You know what your opinions are, and you are good at talking about them. When other people are not sure of the right actions to take, speak up for what you think is right. You can be a spokesperson for others who are afraid to say how they feel.

- You like to think big. Help your friends or groups you are in think big too. They can do more important things with your encouragement. Build their belief in what they can accomplish. Think big. Achieve big.

- Think about taking an active role in a group in your school or community. Your confidence and ability to move forward can help the group be more successful.

- Talk to your counselor or favorite teacher about what you would like to learn in the future and goals you would like to accomplish. Pick out classes or clubs that will help you reach your goals. Use your Confidence talents to keep trying new things.

- You are comfortable making your own path. When other people stop at a roadblock, you find another way. Most times you are successful, but sometimes you are not. When you are disappointed, think about how you can try again or succeed at something else. Your belief in what you can do keeps you going.

Action items for parents of children with **Confidence**

- How can you build on your child's accomplishments and set him up for success? Are there things you know he would be great at that you and he haven't explored yet? Think about the best ways to use his Confidence talents when choosing activities that will lead to more success.

- Confidence talents can lead children into positive or adverse situations because they like to think big and achieve big. Help your child clarify exactly what he wants to achieve and how he can go about it in the best possible way.

- Your child's confidence helps him persevere and come back from disappointments, and it provides him with the fuel to keep going. But be prepared to encourage and support him when necessary. Appreciate his ability to maneuver through situations that many of his peers may not feel comfortable or confident enough to deal with.

Words that describe this theme

director
risk taker
leader

influencer
controlling
independent

certain
self-aware
self-sufficient

Questions for your child

What are you most proud of?

Have you ever spoken up for what you knew was right? What happened?

What is a new thing you would like to try?

What is an accomplishment you are looking forward to?

Theme contrasts

Confidence: You believe in yourself.
Caring: You believe in others.

Confidence: You are certain.
Discoverer: You are curious.

Trust is important to you, and

you care about being seen as

responsible and trustworthy.

People count on you to do

what you say you will do.

When you make a promise,

you mean to keep it.

Dependability

Trust is important to you, and you care about being seen as responsible and trustworthy. People count on you to do what you say you will do. When you make a promise, you mean to keep it.

You like being chosen to be in charge of getting something done because you know it means others see you as dependable and trustworthy. Sometimes, being asked to do more is like getting a reward because it means people believe in you. Maybe you have special chores or responsibilities at home or at school. Whatever job you are given, you want to get it done. Some people might say you act older than other kids your age because you are so responsible. You can be a good example to other people. Earning the praise of teachers and parents for getting things done and doing what is right feels good to you. People count on you to do what you say you will do.

Action items for children with **Dependability**

- Other kids may need more reminders than you do to finish important tasks. See how many things you can get done each day before parents or teachers remind you about them. Take pride in being able to say, "I already did it" when they ask and for doing schoolwork or chores without being told.

- It's important to you that you do what you say you will do. You like to keep your promises, and you understand that keeping them builds trust. Before you make a promise, be sure it is one that you can keep. Build a reputation you are proud of.

- You almost always know the right thing to do. If your friends want to do something that might get them in trouble or hurt someone's feelings, don't go along with it. What could you say to change their minds? Help your friends by setting a good example. You might be surprised that they are glad you spoke up.

- People trust you, so they may tell you things that they don't want others to know. You prove that you deserve their trust by keeping their secrets. But, if you think somebody else needs to know a secret, help your friend be brave and do the right thing. Offer to go with your friend if you think he or she needs help telling someone.

- You like it when others depend on you, and more responsibility gives you the chance to help lots of people. Think about one new responsibility you could take on to help a teacher, parent, coach or neighbor. It could be a weekly job or something you do once. A few ideas are:

  - taking care of a neighbor's pet
  - volunteering to be a crossing guard
  - helping with lunch duty
  - cleaning up a park
  - babysitting
  - mowing lawns, raking leaves or shoveling snow

Action items for parents of children with **Dependability**

- To take responsibility, your child first needs to take psychological ownership. Let her make choices rather than assigning her tasks. What projects would she be excited about owning? Help her generate ideas about new and meaningful opportunities for responsibility.

- Recognize and point out when you see your child taking on more responsibility than others her age. Let her know that you appreciate her hard work, dependability and trustworthiness — and that her sense of responsibility makes a difference.

- Trust your child with your ideas, thoughts and feelings. Be aware that others share their ideas, thoughts and feelings with her as well. Acknowledge her Dependability talents by letting her know that you count on her and that you know others do too.

Words that describe this theme

owner	loyal	committed
responder	driven	independent
volunteer	reliable	

Questions for your child

What are three things you like to get done each day?

How are you a good example to younger kids?

What is one new responsibility you would like to take on at home, at school or in your community?

What is your favorite job to do? Who counts on you to get it done?

Theme contrasts

Dependability: You let yourself down when you don't do something right.
Competing: You let yourself down when you don't win.

Dependability: You keep your promises.
Achieving: You keep your successes clearly in mind.

A thinker and learner, you are

excited about exploring ideas

and making connections.

You like to ask the questions

"How?" and "Why?"

Discoverer

A thinker and learner, you are excited about exploring ideas and making connections. You like to ask the questions "How?" and "Why?"

Questions are in your mind a lot. How does that work? Why did that happen? How did someone figure that out? You are excited to explore new ideas and ask questions so you understand the "how" and "why" of the things you choose to learn. You collect and connect information and ideas. It is fun to be an expert, and when you find a subject or idea you like, you can spend a lot of time exploring it. You might be bored doing things the same way everyone else does because you like to find new ways. Talking with creative thinkers is fun because it sparks even more ideas. People can benefit from your information and ideas when you share them.

Action items for children with **Discoverer**

- Choose one or two subjects that interest you a lot. Research them, and try to become an expert on them. Could you know more about something than anyone else in your grade? You like to explore ideas on your own outside of school, so try to earn credit for your research to boost your grades.

- You are good at figuring out how things work. Create a space of your own where you can take things apart and see how they're made.

- Find people who are interested in the same things as you are and start a conversation with them. You can teach each other what you know and learn to look at ideas in new and different ways. Together, you may discover even more about your shared interests because your ideas connect and lead to new ones.

- Use the Internet to explore your ideas. Make a list of great Internet sites where kids can do research. Share the list with teachers and friends, and add their favorites to it. They will appreciate it, and you will have a growing list of places where you can learn about new things.

- You like to get as much information and knowledge as you can before you begin an activity. Sometimes, when others have an idea, they want to jump in and get started. Be the "voice of reason" who helps them get the facts and learn more first.

Action items for parents of children with **Discoverer**

- Ask your child what he is studying, inside or outside the classroom. Think about how you can support his explorations. Use different approaches like reading, experimenting, constructing, deconstructing and field trips to integrate and deepen his learning. Position yourself as a fellow learner, and let him become the expert.

- Observe and ask your child how he likes to learn. Make the most of his learning style to keep him asking "How?" and "Why?" Can you dedicate a special place where he can build, explore, read or work on his own projects and not have to put them away? Show your interest by watching, asking questions or lending a hand when needed.

- Sometimes your child's interest in a subject can be intense but short-lived. For him, the thrill is in starting something new, so he may be ready to move on to the next exciting project rather than finish an old one. To keep his interest, start with a list of possible subjects to explore, but let him guide the topics and suggest new ones.

Words that describe this theme

explorer	student	studious
expert	curious	inquisitive
learner	interested	passionate

Questions for your child

What is your favorite new idea of the week?

Who is your favorite person to ask questions? What does he or she know a lot about?

What is something you want to learn more about?

If you could design your own class to teach, what would it be about?

Theme contrasts

Discoverer: You want to learn about your world.
Organizer: You want to arrange your world.

Discoverer: You ask questions about what is.
Future Thinker: You ask questions about what could be.

Your mind loves to think

and dream about the future.

You are a person who thinks

about what is possible, not

what is impossible.

Future Thinker

Your mind loves to think and dream about the future. You are a person who thinks about what is possible, not what is impossible.

You like to imagine the life you will have, what new things will be invented and what you will be able to do that you cannot do now. What kind of person will you be? How will the world be different in 10 years or 100 years? What are your dreams? Your visions of the future might be bigger than most people's because thinking big is one of your talents. You like to think about the important things in life, what they mean and how they are connected to each other. Finding meaning is important to you. It is not enough for you to simply concentrate on what you need to do today because your mind needs more adventure than that. You spend time thinking about ideas, not just facts. Thinking big paints pictures of what the future can be.

Action items for children with **Future Thinker**

- The stories and scenes in your mind set the stage for what is possible and allow you to rehearse what you will do in the future. Picture yourself doing what you want to do when you are in high school, college or when you have a job. Where will you be, who will you be talking to, what will you look like and what will you be doing?

- You are a deep thinker. Set aside time for yourself to daydream, create, wonder, explore and connect ideas that you like. Just having time to think is important. You might even have a certain place you can go when you want to think, explore and dream.

- What do you like about the future? What do you think is exciting or possible? Are there comic books, science fiction movies or stories that give you ideas of what the future could be like? How about technology or inventions? Find something to read or do each week that helps you learn more about the future.

- Do you picture yourself as a student council member, tennis player, church youth leader or volunteer someday? Watch what people in those roles do. Think about what you would do or say if you were in their shoes. Playing out conversations and actions in your mind will give you confidence and help you prepare for the future.

- How will your life be different when you are an adult? What do you want to know more about? Asking questions is a great way to think about and plan for the future. Every day, find one good question to ask yourself or another person to learn more about what lies ahead.

Action items for parents of children with **Future Thinker**

- Give your child a chance to verbalize her thoughts about the future. Simply ask questions like, "What do you think you will be doing next year? What about two years from now?" Appreciate and accept her visions for what they are — forward thinking.

- Share your own thoughts, ideas and dreams with your child as you think about what the future might bring. Your sharing will spark her thinking and validate that the future is worthy of conversation.

- As you peer into your child's future, what are the steps you both need to take to accomplish her goals? What do you need to do to prepare? Help her meet people, select activities and explore opportunities that are in line with her visions for the future.

Words that describe this theme

dreamer	visionary	illustrator
imaginative	creative	expressive
hopeful	inspiring	future-oriented

Questions for your child

What are your hopes for your future? What do you think is exciting or possible?

How will your life be different when you are an adult?

What do you think you will be doing next year? What about five years from now?

What is a dream you picture yourself in?

Theme contrasts

Future Thinker: You ask about the future.
Discoverer: You ask about the present.

Future Thinker: You can see a better world.
Organizer: Your world is better when it is organized.

Scheduling, planning and

organizing your world makes

life better. People count on

you to get the details right

and pull a plan together.

Organizer

Clifton Youth
StrengthsExplorer

Scheduling, planning and organizing your world makes life better. People count on you to get the details right and pull a plan together.

You like to create order in your world. Schedules help you feel in control of your life. Planning makes you comfortable and calm about what you are going to do. It is fun to think ahead, organize and include all that you want to do in your plan so you don't leave anything out. You like to think about both the big ideas and the details. It feels good to make something absolutely perfect, whether it is as simple as your hair or as complicated as a big project for school. It is important to you to be on time or even early so you are ready to start whatever you are about to do. Not only do you like order and rules for yourself, you like them for other people too. You help yourself and others by pulling all the pieces together.

Action items for children with **Organizer**

- You like to make a schedule and stick to it. Keep a calendar for yourself so you can look at what you want to do each day and look ahead to the week, month and year coming up. You will feel more in control of your life if you can see it in front of you.

- Planning projects and events feels good to you. If you are working in a group, volunteer to be the planner and organizer. Keep a list of all the things that need to be done and who is supposed to do each one. Organize it by person or by due date, and share your list to help everyone understand the plan.

- A list can help you keep track of what you need to do. Draw a box to the left of each activity on your list. Then, when you finish a task, put a check mark in the box so you can easily see how many things are done and how many are left to do. You might be surprised at how good it feels to check that box and see what you've accomplished.

- You are good at creating order. Find the best ways to organize your school supplies, your locker or your bedroom. Establishing and maintaining neatness makes you feel good and helps you and others find what you need.

- Look around. Who could benefit from how you like to organize? Could you help organize a family event? Would a teacher appreciate the way you can organize papers? Find a way to use your talents to help someone else.

Action items for parents of children with **Organizer**

- Ask your child how he likes to manage his time and if he has ideas for more efficient use of your family's time. Ask him how he would schedule the day, week, weekend, semester break or summer. Then help him implement his ideas and plans.

- Think about how your child can help you or others using his Organizer talents, and find opportunities for him to do so. For instance, at school, could he organize the classroom or science lab or manage the sports equipment? At home, what would be fun for him to plan and arrange — from a junk drawer to a family event?

- Connect your child with someone who is at least two years older and who is good at organizing. Find someone who can model the value of organization. Watching an older Organizer will give him ideas and examples of how to put his talents into action.

Words that describe this theme

structured	detailed	systematic
orderly	planner	rule follower
neat		

Questions for your child

Did you organize anything yesterday? What did you do to bring structure to it?

What is something you like to have just perfect?

Who could benefit from how you like to organize? How would you help him or her?

Are there any activities or events coming up that you want to plan or arrange?

Theme contrasts

Organizer: You arrange the plan.
Achieving: You accomplish the plan.

Organizer: You put all of the pieces together.
Discoverer: You pull all of the pieces apart.

You were born to be at the

front of the room telling

stories and taking the lead.

Other people watch you and

listen to you.

Presence

You were born to be at the front of the room telling stories and taking the lead. Other people watch you and listen to you.

You are a natural at commanding attention. You may do this in small ways or in big ways, but you are better at it than most people, and it gives you power over a group. Sometimes humor is the way you get a group excited. You might tell a funny joke or story that helps others relax and feel connected to each other. Sometimes your leadership is more serious. Maybe there is something important to be done, and you are the spokesperson who can get the message out to people in a way that makes them want to be involved. You might someday be a teacher, a politician, a speaker, a comedian, a preacher or a business leader. Whatever you choose to be, you are likely to have others listening to the words you speak. You naturally create an audience.

Action items for children with **Presence** ———————

- People seem to pay attention to you. The way you talk about others and the activities you take part in can influence people. Think about how you can use your Presence talents to make a positive difference and make your class, your school or your community better.

- There are many ways to get attention and to get others to listen. Ask people you know for ideas about how to connect with an audience. What works best? Speaking fast, slow, loud, soft or with a pause? Consider being the host, master of ceremonies or narrator for a program so you can practice.

- Laughter is good for people. What kind of humor do you want to be known for — the kind that makes everybody feel good or the kind that hurts others? Every time you have an audience — your friends, your family or even your class listening to a book report — use humor that builds people up rather than brings them down.

- Do you want to be a great speaker, actor or presenter? Who have you seen in person, on TV or in a video that everyone really liked? When you see those people, notice what they do well, and see if the same things work for you when you speak or present.

- Talking, speaking or acting in front of a group is scary to a lot of people. Practice a speech, joke or story over and over again to help you gain confidence. You might feel nervous inside when you speak to a group, but others will not notice, especially if you practice.

Action items for parents of children with **Presence** ———

- Be your child's audience, whether it's one on one in the kitchen or in a crowded auditorium. She wants a reaction. Applaud, laugh and ask for encores. Find others who appreciate her talent for performing. Could she call Grandma to share a joke? Could you invite another person into the room? Could she teach a class? Some ideas for her to put her talent into action are:
  - taking performance-related classes or lessons, for example, singing, acting or dancing

- joining speech, choir, band or drama
- performing in variety or talent shows or at birthday parties, holiday celebrations, assemblies, sporting events, nursing homes, family gatherings or places of worship

• Recap the highlights of your child's performances — big or small — and point out others' positive responses: their facial expressions, gestures and body language. Praise her comedic timing or dramatic pauses. Affirm her well-chosen words. Whether her performance is brilliant or mediocre, emphasize the best of what she did.

• Encourage your child to practice her card trick, song or book report so it keeps getting better. Give her room to try out her material.

Words that describe this theme

performer	aspiring	visible
outgoing	admired	influential
star	successful	

Questions for your child

How do you know when people are really listening to you? What do you do to make them pay attention?

Have you made anyone laugh in the past week? What did you do or say that was funny?

Who are your favorite people to watch or listen to? What do you like about how they perform?

What would you like to get better at doing? Who can help you rehearse?

Theme contrasts

Presence: You want to be seen and heard.
Discoverer: You want to question and learn.

Presence: You want attention.
Competing: You want to win.

You like to start friendships

and keep them for a long

time — maybe even your

whole life. You widen the

circle of friends for yourself

and others.

Relating

You like to start friendships and keep them for a long time — maybe even your whole life. You widen the circle of friends for yourself and others.

There are many ways to be good at relating. You might easily meet new people, learn their names and make friends very quickly wherever you go. You might take time to make friends but be good at building long-lasting friendships. You might do both. If you make friends quickly, people probably view you as happy, outgoing and instantly likeable. If you would rather spend time with a small group of friends talking, laughing or just being together, these friends might see you as a best friend they can trust and talk to. You might be best at relating with teachers, parents and other adults, and they can help you learn and feel good about yourself. Whatever your style of relating, people like you, and relationships are important to you.

Action items for children with **Relating**

- Friends are an important part of your world. Do you want to make some of your friendships stronger? Make a point of inviting those friends to do things with you or to spend time with your other friends. Get to know their family, pets or hobbies. Let them get to know you too. The more time you spend together, the better friends you can become.

- Beginning friendships can be fun and quick for you. One way to start a friendship is by simply saying hi and learning someone's name. Each week, try to get to know one person better. Learn the person's name and find out something new about him or her each day. Find something that both of you like.

- Challenge yourself to see how many people's names you can learn in your school or class. Keep a list of the names you learn each week. As the list grows, so will your circle of friends.

- When people are in a new situation, like when they are at a new school or when they don't know anyone at a party, they probably feel nervous. You can help by quickly welcoming them, asking their names and introducing them to your friends. They will feel better when they feel like they have friends too.

- When you give someone a compliment and say you like something about him or her, you make that person's day better. And it probably makes you both feel good about each other. Try to compliment at least two people each day. It might be as simple as saying, "Thanks for lending me a pencil" or, "Nice shoes" as someone walks down the hall.

Action items for parents of children with **Relating**

- Ask your child about his friends. Honor his Relating talents by letting him talk about what's going on with other kids. Listening is affirming. Offer advice only when he asks for it.

- Relationships come in all shapes and sizes. How does your child relate best — one on one or in groups? Does he interact best with younger children, peers or adults? Encourage his talent for building relationships, and create opportunities for interactions. For example, when you go on an outing, have him bring along a friend. Arrange study groups that include him. Consider asking him to help younger children.

- Remember that your child's reaction to the world is filtered through relationships. Interactions throughout the day will affect his mood. Don't take it personally. Understand, acknowledge and listen to his feelings, and appreciate his interpretations.

Words that describe this theme

friend	greeter	team player
connector	teacher	likeable
inclusive	approachable	

Questions for your child

How long you have known your closest friend?

Have you complimented any of your friends recently? Is there someone you could compliment more in the future?

What are two questions you could ask someone you would like to know better to know more about what he or she is like?

How could you learn the names of more kids in your class or in other classes?

Theme contrasts

Relating: You connect with people.
Discoverer: You connect with thoughts and ideas.

Relating: You establish friendships.
Competing: You establish wins.

A 23-year longitudinal study

of 1,000 children in New

Zealand found that a child's

personality at age

3 shows remarkable

similarity to his or her

reported personality

traits at age 26.

StrengthsSpotting

The next time you walk into a room with several very young children who don't know you well, notice how they respond to you. One freezes and watches you intently. Another begins crying. One ignores you and keeps playing. One makes eye contact and smiles, just waiting for your response. And chances are good that those children will act the same way the next time a new person walks in. Even at an early age, people show their individuality.

Gallup created the Clifton StrengthsFinder assessment for adults and kids who are 15 years old and older and the Clifton Youth StrengthsExplorer assessment for children who are 10-14. But what about children who are under the age of 10? Because these children are so young, Gallup doesn't have an online assessment they can take that reveals their talents.

Instead, StrengthsSpotting is Gallup's model for finding talents in children who are younger than 10 years old. It is based on the Clifton Youth StrengthsExplorer and relies on repeated observations of young children in a variety of settings and interactions.

One of the easiest ways to begin the quest of discovering your young child's talents is by just watching her in many different settings — with a play group, with siblings or neighbors, in a sandbox, on the soccer field, in a classroom, or at music lessons. As you consciously observe your child, you will start to gain insights into how she spontaneously thinks, feels and acts. You are likely to see her exhibit a variety of behaviors and reactions. However, the more times you observe the same response across different settings, the more likely it may be a budding talent.

Like older kids and adults, very young children will have unique reactions depending on their individual talents. And as you observe and listen, you can see them display their natural inclinations. I was watching a group of 7-year-olds play baseball one hot evening. One little guy walked away visibly upset after his team lost the game. He was repeatedly ramming his bat into the ground. His dad reached over to give him a reassuring hug, but the boy pulled away and walked ahead. Ten feet behind him, another child from the same team was leaving with his mom. But that boy was happily skipping toward the car saying, "I love playing with my friends. Is it time for ice cream?" Both kids were on the same field playing the same game for the same team, but they reacted to the loss very differently — even at 7 years old.

Just as your child's reactions can be key indicators of his talents, his favorite activities or interests give you another clue to his talents. What does he love to do? What captures his attention? It might be bugs, cars, baby dolls, books, baseball, a keyboard, painting or lots of other things. Or, maybe your child is determined to master a developmental stage — walking, learning to ride a tricycle or hopping on one leg. By the time your child is verbal, not only can you observe, you can simply ask. Paying attention to his interests can be valuable as you consider ways to encourage his development. And, when you need to teach your child a new concept or reinforce something with him, using his interests can expedite the process.

Diann, a preschool teacher, explains: "Think of it this way: What is something you as a grown-up enjoy doing and are naturally good at? I love arts and crafts, and I'm a creative learner. When I get to use my creative energy, I get excited. My senses are more alive, and I am much more interested in learning something new that will help me with my creativity. On the other hand, I don't like math. I use it as little as possible and only to get by. I have to balance my checkbook and pay bills. Those are tasks I have to do. But when I'm doing something creative, I don't mind math at all because it helps me do what I want to do. I need to figure out yardage for fabric or the number of colored rocks I need for a mosaic, but I don't dread doing the math because the project has my interest piqued. At times like that, I am my most authentic self because I am engaged in the creative thing I am doing. Wouldn't that be true for a 1-year-old, 6-year-old or teenager?"

So let's say your child loves football. If Diann wanted to help him learn math, she would ask him questions like, "If a team scores two touchdowns and makes an extra point, what is their score?" If your child is younger and just learning numbers, Diann might use little footballs for counting. If she was helping him with reading, she could offer him books or articles about his favorite team.

To give you an idea of how young children might exhibit their natural talents and interests within the context of the 10 Clifton Youth StrengthsExplorer themes, picture a group of kids playing at the park. Depending on the age and maturity level of the children, you might see something like this:

- **Achieving:** Achieving children are self-starters who love to get things done. This child walks onto the playground and starts figuring out how many pieces of playground equipment he can play on.

- **Caring:** Caring children are fulfilled by helping and encouraging others. This child helps someone who needs a boost onto the monkey bars or rushes over to help the child who scrapes his knee.

- **Competing:** Competing children strive to win and see many activities as contests. This child races to get the first swing and pumps it higher than anyone else.

- **Confidence:** Confidence children enjoy trying something no one else is doing and feel confident they will be able to take on the task at hand. When the others warily eye the tall slide, this child is the first to step up and give it a try.

- **Dependability:** Children with Dependability like to be trusted and held responsible for getting things done. This child takes responsibility for making sure that when it's time to leave the park, he has everything packed up that he brought.

- **Discoverer:** Discoverers are excited about making connections, exploring and asking "How?" and "Why?" As this child goes up the climbing wall, she wonders how many different ways she could get to the top.

- **Future Thinker:** Future Thinkers like to think about what is coming next and imagine where they will be in the future. This child climbs to the top of the rocket ship and begins pretending he's an astronaut.

- **Organizer:** Organizers like to plan and to create structure and order. This child arranges for everyone to take turns. She makes sure to number everyone and get them lined up in order.

- **Presence:** Children with Presence love to be the center of attention. Hanging upside down from the monkey bars isn't enough for this child. He probably yells, "Watch me!" or makes monkey noises too.

- **Relating:** Relating children are good at starting and maintaining friendships. This child is the one who says, "Hey, let's go up the slide together!" or, "Come on. Let's climb the wall together."

Remember, the best way to start discovering your young child's talents is by observing her in a variety of situations and settings over time. Watch for glimpses of excellence — moments when you are amazed at how well she does something or when she surprises you or herself. As you start to look for early signs of talent in your young child, keep these guidelines in mind:

1. Familiarize yourself with the 10 Clifton Youth StrengthsExplorer themes: Achieving, Caring, Competing, Confidence, Dependability, Discoverer, Future Thinker, Organizer, Presence and Relating. Consider how children who aren't quite ready for the Clifton Youth StrengthsExplorer assessment yet might start to exhibit these themes. Use them to help you categorize your observations of your child.

2. Watch for clues to talent. Note when your child displays:

   - **Yearnings:** What activities or environments is your child repeatedly drawn to or eager to try?

   - **Rapid learning:** What new skills or activities does your child pick up quickly and easily?

- **Satisfaction:** When is your child most enthusiastic and fulfilled? Which activities is she excited about doing again and again?
- **Timelessness:** When does your child become so engrossed that she seems to lose track of time?

3. Collaborate with others who know and care about your child. Discuss the specific patterns you have spotted in her with them to test the accuracy of your observations. Ask them what patterns they have seen, and compare notes.

4. Identify the patterns you see most often. Through repeated observations over time, you can determine which ones are dominant. Make these patterns the focus of your child's ongoing development.

5. Create opportunities for developing your child's talents. As much as you can, guide or arrange activities that make the most of your child's interests and talents.

6. Build a network of "StrengthsSpotters." Share pictures and stories of your child doing what she does best with others who care about her and who are invested in her — for example, your spouse, grandparents, teachers and other caregivers.

As you focus on your young child's natural inclinations and interests, you will continue to learn more about who she is and who she will become. And talking with others will give you further insight that will reinforce or redirect your observations. Once you understand what's important to and for your child, you can set the stage for successful, happy moments that create building blocks for the future.

LEARN MORE ABOUT STRENGTHSSPOTTING

Recommended age level:
Children younger than 10

StrengthsSpotting is Gallup's model for finding talents in children who are younger than 10. StrengthsSpotting uses the 10 Clifton Youth StrengthsExplorer themes as a foundation, combined with repeated observations of young children in a variety of settings and interactions.

As you observe your child's talents in greater detail, read this section for each Clifton Youth StrengthsExplorer theme's definition, clues that your child is exhibiting emerging signs of the theme, action items for you and snapshots of children who exhibit the theme.

You have more energy

and more goals than other

people. You love a sense

of accomplishment.

Achieving

You have more energy and more goals than other people. You love a sense of accomplishment.

You are in a hurry to get started and make things happen because you almost always have a list in your mind of the things you want to get done. It is fun to achieve small goals and even more exciting to achieve big goals that challenge you. The more you get done, the more you feel like a successful person. And the more successes you have, the more you want to have. Finishing a project feels good to you because you love a sense of accomplishment. An award, a good grade or praise can mean a lot to you because it feels good when your effort and ability are noticed. Because you are a hard worker, you always feel that you could and should be doing more.

Does your young child exhibit emerging signs of the **Achieving** theme?

- All children are wired to learn and grow and like to be acknowledged for their successes, but Achieving children thrive on this acknowledgement. And the more specific the praise, the more it means to them. Achieving children would rather not have to ask for recognition, but they will, because it is the icing on the cake and a signal that they are done and can move on to the next challenge.

- Achieving children have energy that they may display physically, emotionally or cognitively. And they like to have challenging ways to use that energy. These children are self-starters, so they will find something every day to achieve. They are naturally active. Remember that there are different types of activity, so they may not be running around the room, but instead might be cognitively active and have several toys out to play with.

- While Achieving children do get energized by accomplishment, there might be times when they will not start something if it's too overwhelming or they feel they can't complete it.

Action items for parents

- Your Achieving child has a lot of energy. This energy can be physical, cognitive, emotional or any combination. Give her opportunities and choices to use her energy — lots of them. Making her own choices may help her develop her sense of direction.

- Make a list with your Achieving child of a few things she would like to do each day. At the end of the day, remind her of the list and check off with her what she did or didn't accomplish. You can be a role model for her by sharing a few of the things you got done as well.

- When your Achieving child is working on something, she will likely be "in the zone." Realize that she might not hear you because she is concentrating and fulfilling her Achieving talents.

Snapshots of an **Achieving** child

Rohan is goal-oriented and can concentrate on tasks and projects longer than most of his friends. When he decides what he is going to do, he sticks with it no matter how difficult it is. For example, as a preschooler, he loved puzzles and worked diligently until he mastered each one. He would stack them up as he completed them, and he knew exactly which ones he would work on every day. As a 9-year-old, Rohan was happiest when there was a lot going on and he knew what he needed to do. His best way to start each day is to check the calendar on the refrigerator to see what he needs to accomplish. He is at his best when he is busy and productive — otherwise, he can quickly complain that he's bored.

In your heart, helping other

people is very important.

You want to make the world

better by helping people in

small ways or big ways.

Caring

In your heart, helping other people is very important. You want to make the world better by helping people in small ways or big ways.

You have a big heart. You feel good when you reach out and help people. You are the friend who includes others. When someone feels left out, you help him or her be part of your group. It is easy for you to encourage people, share with them and help them learn. You know you have something to offer other people. Even the smallest kind deed is important in people's everyday lives. Whether you help in big or small ways, you can make a difference in your world. People count on you to be kind, thoughtful and caring.

Does your young child exhibit emerging signs of the **Caring** theme?

- Children strong in the Caring theme will often help others without being asked. When they do, they do it with a warm, kind spirit. And they *will* help other children, even if the other children might not want help.

- Caring children may create ways to help their peers, and sometimes they seek out younger children to care for. Some Caring children transfer their attention to dolls, stuffed animals, pets or adults.

- Caring kids radiate joy and are fulfilled when they are in their element — caring for and helping others. Because they want to help and are sensitive to other people, they may also express concern, sadness or distress when others are sad or struggling, especially if they can't comfort those who are hurting.

Action items for parents

- Find people your Caring child can help — siblings, friends, teachers, classmates or neighbors. Give him tasks to help you and others. If he is a bit older, let him assist with younger children.

- Make sure all recipients actually need and want help from your Caring child. Help him build this talent into a strength by being a role model and by giving him ideas for how to make a positive impact that is right for each person he helps.

- Be sure to let your Caring child know when and how his caring matters. Depending on his age and the situation, it might be as simple as telling him, "You are such a good helper!" or, "I like the way you are taking care of the puppy."

Snapshots of a **Caring** child

When Jasmine was 2 years old, she was tuned into the feelings of those around her. When others got rowdy, Jasmine would scream. She recognized the feelings but didn't understand how to deal with them. When a friend was sad, she would hand him a toy. In preschool, for example, if a friend tripped and fell, Jasmine would hug her and say, "Are you better now?" In elementary school, Jasmine would come home every day and slump over. She looked like she was carrying the weight of the world on her shoulders. She was. While she was doing well in school herself, she wanted to take care of her friends who were feeling bad or had hurt feelings, but as a fifth-grader, she didn't always know how. When there was conflict, Jasmine would remove herself from the situation and retreat from her friends. When her mom started asking her how the day had gone and how her friends were, Jasmine could talk about her feelings as her mom listened. Then, together they could sort through how Jasmine could help. As Jasmine has gotten older, she loves babysitting for the neighbors and volunteering for community activities.

You see many things in life as

a game, and you feel great

joy when you win. You truly

hate to lose because you are

always striving for first place.

Competing

You see many things in life as a game, and you feel great joy when you win. You truly hate to lose because you are always striving for first place.

Every day you compete. Winning first place is your goal in any contest that you feel is worth your time. If there is no one to compete against, you compete against yourself to do more or accomplish a goal faster or better. You can be competing against someone else even when that person doesn't know it. Because you hate to lose, you might get angry, upset or even cry. It does not matter if others think the contest is important. If you are doing it, you want to be number one. Others look to you for the motivation to win.

Does your young child exhibit emerging signs of the **Competing** theme?

- Competing children pay attention to what others are doing and try to imitate them — and ultimately may outdo them. They might compete with siblings or others for your attention. They will race other children to be first to any activity or destination. Winning is wonderful, but losing is not an option.

- In an attempt to win, Competing kids may jump in before they understand an activity or listen to the rules.

- Competing children may be fidgety until they can compete. They thrive on winning and usually are competing, even if others aren't aware they're in a contest. Often they will create ways to compete with others. You can tell they are competing just by the way they carry themselves and by the fire in their eyes to win.

Action items for parents

- Give your Competing child ideas for how to compete with herself — "You did five situps last time. Let's see if you can do seven this time." — or with a clock — "Can you finish by the time the second hand is on the three?"

- Document your Competing child's accomplishments. For example, make a chart with star stickers or display photos of her wins. Ask her what her next goal will be. If she is on a team, help her consider both personal and team wins.

- When your Competing child competes, determine when and how to celebrate her wins. Recognition will motivate her to reach higher levels. As she develops this talent, you will have many chances to help her refine it. Sometimes, you may need to persuade her to consider her responses to others.

Snapshots of a **Competing** child

Marcus thinks every person he meets wants to race him, challenge him and keep score — whether it is who can tie his shoes first, learning to ride a bike, building the highest tower of blocks, playing a video game, shooting hoops on the basketball court or being the first to get a project done. Marcus is focused on being the first and best. It is what motivates him. When he was younger, he needed to be told more frequently than the other preschoolers that he had to wait his turn. And there were a few tears whenever he lost a competition. Now that he is a bit older, Marcus can regulate his competitive instinct better, but he still thinks most activities can be turned into win/lose situations. As a middle school student, he is more into sports than studies, and he excels in classes where he is given a clear and measurable challenge.

You believe in yourself and

what you can do. This helps

you take on challenges

because you feel sure you

can succeed.

Confidence

You believe in yourself and what you can do. This helps you take on challenges because you feel sure you can succeed.

Because you are confident, you are able to do things that others may not want to try. Knowing that you are a unique and special person in the world gives you the power to be who you are. You don't have to be like everybody else, and you don't have to follow the crowd. Even when you don't feel it, other people may see you as brave because you will speak up even if no one else will. You are sure enough of your opinions that you will take a stand for them. It is great to believe in what you can do because this belief helps you do more in your life.

Does your young child exhibit emerging signs of the Confidence theme?

- Confidence children are secure in their abilities and believe in themselves. They don't seem to get flustered or upset when they are working on a new task or goal.

- Children with Confidence enjoy trying something no one else will. They feel they are capable of handling whatever they're doing. They might be the first to volunteer or try something without help from an adult or another child.

- You can tell when children with Confidence are in a state of flow. Their voice, face and body language will reflect their inner certainty.

Action items for parents

- Remember that even though your child with Confidence is exceptionally sure of himself, he may feel insecure in some areas. Watch his eyes, body language and tone so you know when he needs help.

- Allow your Confidence child to build on his past accomplishments. He is sure of his ability to succeed, so have stimulating activities available to challenge him. Give him choices you approve of for these activities, but let him decide which ones to pursue.

- Let your Confidence child experiment, and give him opportunities to shine. Don't jump in too soon when he is trying to solve a problem or learn a new skill; he will want to try it by himself first.

Snapshots of a **Confidence** child

Even as a 3-year-old, Miguel was confident. If his teacher needed someone to demonstrate a new skill or volunteer, he was willing to give it a shot. On the day Miguel rode the bus to school for the very first time, the bus driver didn't notice him sitting in the back of the bus. It wasn't until the driver got to the bus barn that he saw Miguel. Miguel was a little upset, but the next day, he marched back onto the bus, confident it wouldn't happen again. When he was at the swimming pool and the lifeguard demonstrated a flip off the diving board, even though Miguel had never tried it, he was the first one to do a flip. And now in middle school, when all of his friends sit at the same lunch table every day and eat hot lunches, he confidently brings his sack lunch from home.

Trust is important to you, and

you care about being seen as

responsible and trustworthy.

People count on you to do

what you say you will do.

When you make a promise,

you mean to keep it.

Dependability

Trust is important to you, and you care about being seen as responsible and trustworthy. People count on you to do what you say you will do. When you make a promise, you mean to keep it.

You like being chosen to be in charge of getting something done because you know it means others see you as dependable and trustworthy. Sometimes, being asked to do more is like getting a reward because it means people believe in you. Maybe you have special chores or responsibilities at home or at school. Whatever job you are given, you want to get it done. Some people might say you act older than other kids your age because you are so responsible. You can be a good example to other people. Earning the praise of teachers and parents for getting things done and doing what is right feels good to you. People count on you to do what you say you will do.

Does your young child exhibit emerging signs of the **Dependability** theme?

- Children with Dependability love to be trusted to do things on their own, like delivering messages to others or walking the dog alone.

- Dependability children follow through on responsibilities or promises they make. If they say they will do something, they most likely complete the activity.

- Taking on a responsibility is important to Dependability children, and having just one responsibility probably isn't enough. After taking on an activity or job they have been given, they are eager for another.

Action items for parents

- Find lots of ways to give your Dependability child developmentally appropriate responsibility that will let her know you count on her. She will feel especially important if you ask her what chores or responsibilities she would like to take on.

- Your Dependability child likes to have choices, so give her options — "Would you like to color this now or after lunch?" Once she commits to the option she chooses, she'll be sure to get it done.

- Give your Dependability child structure, security and routine. She will come back every now and then to make sure the rules are still the same so that she knows she is doing what you expect of her. She's probably not challenging you but just double checking that she is on course.

Snapshots of a **Dependability** child

In preschool, Lauren loved the "water room." One day when she and her classmates were playing, the windows in the water room fogged up and the kids couldn't see through them. Lauren's teacher gave her a towel to wipe the steam off the windows. She wiped and cleared every window before she went back to playing. Because her teacher had given her a responsibility, this little 3-year-old kept checking the windows and would wipe them down as they steamed up. It was her duty. In elementary school, teachers always counted on her to take messages to the office. Others relied on her to collect money for fundraisers and to assist friends who asked for help with activities. In middle school, Lauren knows a lot about others because they confide in her, and they know that she will keep their secrets.

A thinker and learner, you are

excited about exploring ideas

and making connections.

You like to ask the questions

"How?" and "Why?"

Discoverer

A thinker and learner, you are excited about exploring ideas and making connections. You like to ask the questions "How?" and "Why?"

Questions are in your mind a lot. How does that work? Why did that happen? How did someone figure that out? You are excited to explore new ideas and ask questions so you understand the "how" and "why" of the things you choose to learn. You collect and connect information and ideas. It is fun to be an expert, and when you find a subject or idea you like, you can spend a lot of time exploring it. You might be bored doing things the same way everyone else does because you like to find new ways. Talking with creative thinkers is fun because it sparks even more ideas. People can benefit from your information and ideas when you share them.

Does your young child exhibit emerging signs of the **Discoverer** theme?

- Discoverer children become excited when they figure something out. They are naturally curious and want to know more. They will take the time to study — a sport, a bug, a book, water in the fountain or sink, another child's hair — whatever interests them.

- Children with Discoverer often tune out the rest of the world when they are studying something interesting. They get a thrill out of making connections and learning. These connections are their fuel.

- Discoverer children may study an activity before starting it. They might be extremely deliberative and may even get labeled as slow when they are actually processing different ways to complete a task.

Action items for parents

- Your Discoverer child will find new and interesting ways to do things. Respect his creative process. He may want to put his own twist on an activity because he is bored doing it the way he already knows. Honor that, and let him. This is how he builds his personal connections to himself, other people and his environment.

- Give your Discoverer child novel ways to discover and connect every day. Read a book using different voices, or put new words in an old song — the activity doesn't have to be elaborate, but it does have to be different.

- Your Discoverer child thrives on stimulation. Don't squash his inner Discoverer talents by dictating steps or methods. Where an activity goes is up to him because he will have questions. He'll learn his own way, and he needs the freedom to change things around.

Snapshots of a **Discoverer** child

Why, why, why, is Avni's motto. While curiosity is a typical developmental stage in the very young, asking why is how Avni learns and discovers. When she was learning her letters, her mom said, "A is for Avni and B is for Betsy and C is for Cameron." Avni's mom thought that was enough letters for a not-quite-3-year-old, but Avni demanded, "What is D for? What is E for? What is F for?" Avni was delighted to find that she could match each letter with someone's name. When her second-grade science teacher did the well-known experiment of dropping a mint candy into a soda bottle, Avni was entranced by the explanation as much as by the explosion. Avni isn't interested in being the world's best chemist, at least not yet. She doesn't care what projects look like in the end as much as she enjoys the process of creating them. For example, if you ask her about an art project, Avni will explain how she created it, rather than what the picture is. For her, the fun is in the experiment, not the result.

Your mind loves to think

and dream about the future.

You are a person who thinks

about what is possible, not

what is impossible.

Future Thinker

Your mind loves to think and dream about the future. You are a person who thinks about what is possible, not what is impossible.

You like to imagine the life you will have, what new things will be invented and what you will be able to do that you cannot do now. What kind of person will you be? How will the world be different in 10 years or 100 years? What are your dreams? Your visions of the future might be bigger than most people's because thinking big is one of your talents. You like to think about the important things in life, what they mean and how they are connected to each other. Finding meaning is important to you. It is not enough for you to simply concentrate on what you need to do today because your mind needs more adventure than that. You spend time thinking about ideas, not just facts. Thinking big paints pictures of what the future can be.

Does your young child exhibit emerging signs of the **Future Thinker** theme?

- Future Thinker children like to envision who they might be and what they might do. They may spend time role playing their future actions, jobs and responsibilities. They might also talk about what older kids or adults are doing and ask questions.

- It's important to recognize that the future isn't the same thing to children as it is to adults. To an adult, the future may be five years from now. To a 2-year-old, the future is when she wakes up from her nap; to an 8-year-old, the future may be when he starts a new grade in school. No matter how they define the "future," it is where kids with Future Thinker talents spend a lot of their mental energy.

- Sometimes Future Thinker children may appear to be ignoring those around them, but they're really thinking about what's coming up. Their pondering might be misinterpreted as "spacing out," when in reality, they're thinking about lunch, what they will do this summer or what shoes to wear for basketball practice.

Action items for parents

- At different ages and stages, find ways for your Future Thinker child to explore who she can be in the future. Find role models who embody her interests and talents. For example, if she likes music or playing an instrument, look for kids involved in music who are a few years older. Let her watch and talk with them about how they got where they are and what they love about it.

- Role playing and creating scenarios is a great way for your young Future Thinker to practice what she might do in the future. For example, encourage her to "play school" if she thinks about being a teacher someday. Set up a space for her where she can make lesson plans and rehearse them.

- Ask your Future Thinker child what she has been dreaming about. Kids who are strong in this area have movies playing in their minds of adventures, activities and even jobs they like to think about. Appreciate her ideas and visions by listening to her and helping her make them a reality if and when appropriate.

Snapshots of a **Future Thinker** child

Andre has lots of ideas about the future. In preschool, he collaborated with his friends to act out a show about who they wanted to be when they grew up. He was always thinking ahead, pretending and envisioning himself as a Blues Brother, wearing sunglasses and singing on stage. Before that, he was a superhero saving the world. A month later, in kindergarten, Andre had decided to be a fireman. As he got older, Andre explored his interests in a variety of ways because he wanted to figure out how they might be a part of his future life. His interest in music and performing is powerful, so he started playing the saxophone in middle school. He's already thinking about joining the high school band and wants to be ready.

Scheduling, planning and

organizing your world makes

life better. People count on

you to get the details right

and pull a plan together.

Organizer

Scheduling, planning and organizing your world makes life better. People count on you to get the details right and pull a plan together.

You like to create order in your world. Schedules help you feel in control of your life. Planning makes you comfortable and calm about what you are going to do. It is fun to think ahead, organize and include all that you want to do in your plan so you don't leave anything out. You like to think about both the big ideas and the details. It feels good to make something absolutely perfect, whether it is as simple as your hair or as complicated as a big project for school. It is important to you to be on time or even early so you are ready to start whatever you are about to do. Not only do you like order and rules for yourself, you like them for other people too. You help yourself and others by pulling all the pieces together.

Does your young child exhibit emerging signs of the **Organizer** theme?

- When the toy trains are in a straight line or the soccer bags are placed neatly by the bench, Organizer children are at their best. They notice clutter and things that are out of place and want to make adjustments. When their portion of the world is organized, it is easier for them to proceed. Order helps them make sense of their environment and their thought process.

- Organizer children thrive and grow in a tidy environment. These children like having things where they belong. When something is sticking out of a drawer, they will fix it so the drawer shuts. If someone's locker door is open at school, they shut it. Once chaos is banished, they are visibly relieved.

- While having things in place is important for Organizer children, having plans in place is too. They function better when they know the order of activities and when arrangements are made ahead of time.

Action items for parents

- Label bookshelves and toy storage areas to show your Organizer child that you understand his need for order. Keep his play area fairly tidy. When you need to change or move things around, take him on a tour of the room so he can acquaint himself with the new normal and assure himself that things are different but not chaotic.

- Your Organizer child might get upset if his routine changes. He needs order to feel some control and confidence in his day. For him, schedules and routines are extremely important, so make sure your expectations and responses are consistent.

- Before leaving a room, help your Organizer child clean up. He may not want to leave the room until it is in order. Remember that your idea of organization probably isn't the same as your child's.

Snapshots of an **Organizer** child

Ethan likes the world to be orderly, and he likes making it that way. When he was little, he loved to line up all of his cars side by side and sometimes even by color. He usually had only the toys out that he would play with and always put them away in the same place. He thrived on daily routine and was always quick to question his mom if she deviated from it. As a preschooler, he needed a chaos-free world and to keep all his "ducks in a row" … and those ducks were his friends. When a friend or two lagged behind in line at school, Ethan's need for structure kicked in, and he would literally push them back into the line. As he got older, Ethan's planning helped him get his schoolwork completed. He now makes sure that he knows the timelines for his assignments and asks his teachers for clarity so he knows what to expect before going to school.

You were born to be at the

front of the room telling

stories and taking the lead.

Other people watch you and

listen to you.

Presence

You were born to be at the front of the room telling stories and taking the lead. Other people watch you and listen to you.

You are a natural at commanding attention. You may do this in small ways or in big ways, but you are better at it than most people, and it gives you power over a group. Sometimes humor is the way you get a group excited. You might tell a funny joke or story that helps others relax and feel connected to each other. Sometimes your leadership is more serious. Maybe there is something important to be done, and you are the spokesperson who can get the message out to people in a way that makes them want to be involved. You might someday be a teacher, a politician, a speaker, a comedian, a preacher or a business leader. Whatever you choose to be, you are likely to have others listening to the words you speak. You naturally create an audience.

Does your young child exhibit emerging signs of the **Presence** theme?

- Presence children will make a grand entrance — I'M HERE! — no matter where they go. They usually get attention from others because they simply command it.

- Children with Presence thrive by being the center of attention. Their eyes light up, and they may be almost giddy with all the attention they receive.

- Sometimes the attention-seeking behaviors of children with Presence aren't socially ideal; it takes time and experience to learn how to elicit positive attention. Their presence and behaviors are often very entertaining, and they can attract others to their circle.

Action items for parents

- Whether waving and smiling, telling stories and jokes, or demonstrating a skill, communicating with others energizes your Presence child. Think about how you can be the best audience for her. Who else would like to be her audience?

- Your child with Presence gives and gets a lot of energy from other people; she radiates it. Find opportunities for her to release her energy, and let her shine. Give her the freedom to bask in the attention she will get.

- Consider how your child with Presence could teach by example — showing other kids how to stop bullying, how to throw a ball or how to perform dance steps, for example. Others seem to follow your child's lead and will pay attention to her.

Snapshots of a **Presence** child

Mia is the one who makes everyone smile as they watch school programs. She stands in the center of the group, sings the loudest, knows all the actions to the songs, and thrives on smiles and applause. She's expressive, tells captivating stories, and knows how to engage young and old. She was like this as a 3-year-old, as an 8-year-old and as a 13-year old. She is charming, but sometimes her need for attention can overwhelm others. As she got older, Mia found an outlet for her Presence talents by volunteering to read stories to younger classes. She quickly became a favorite. And she took her love for dance and began performing on stage in recitals and competitions.

You like to start friendships

and keep them for a long

time — maybe even your

whole life. You widen the

circle of friends for yourself

and others.

Relating

You like to start friendships and keep them for a long time — maybe even your whole life. You widen the circle of friends for yourself and others.

There are many ways to be good at relating. You might easily meet new people, learn their names and make friends very quickly wherever you go. You might take time to make friends but be good at building long-lasting friendships. You might do both. If you make friends quickly, people probably view you as happy, outgoing and instantly likeable. If you would rather spend time with a small group of friends talking, laughing or just being together, these friends might see you as a best friend they can trust and talk to. You might be best at relating with teachers, parents and other adults, and they can help you learn and feel good about yourself. Whatever your style of relating, people like you, and relationships are important to you.

Does your young child exhibit emerging signs of the **Relating** theme?

- Relating children thrive in an environment where they have friends, and they'll seek out those environments. They may watch other kids closely — not to compete or imitate but to get to know them. They want to make a connection, and they are more animated and happy when they're interacting with a friend.

- Relating children won't be the first to charge out the door; they'll wait for other children to come along.

- Relating children may be willing to share or give a toy to another child because that is one way they connect and form bonds. They light up when they make a connection or when someone returns their friendship.

Action items for parents

- Playing and learning with others is important for your Relating child. Find out who his best friends are, and make arrangements for them to get together. Learn the names of the children in his classroom, on his teams and in your neighborhood.

- Your Relating child may prefer one-on-one interactions, a very small group or "the more the merrier." Watch not only whom he prefers to relate with but how. Find out his favorite ways to relate to others, and give him plenty of opportunities to make connections.

- Help your Relating child grow his circle of friends and his ability to build friendships. Encourage him to learn others' names and to find something each one is interested in or likes to do. Even a very young Relating child will quickly pick up on making connections with others.

Snapshots of a **Relating** child

When she was 2, Gabriella made sure that each of her friends had a place to sit down on the play mat and no one was left out. If she didn't know someone's name, she simply asked what it was. Then, whenever she said hi, she included that person's name. When Gabriella was 7, she asked if she could have the seat by the door at her after-school program. That way, she could greet each person who entered the room — kids and adults. She was quiet but welcomed others with her smile. When she was 12, Gabriella became a welcome ambassador at her church. She introduces new youth group members to each other and makes a point of including them in the group's projects. She prefers to learn new things in small groups.

References

Introduction

Dovey, D. (2015, May 22). Nature vs. nurture debate: 50-year twin study proves it takes two to determine human traits. Medical Daily. Retrieved August 18, 2015, from http://www.medicaldaily.com/nature-vs-nurture-debate-50-year-twin-study-proves-it-takes-two-determine-human-334686

Genetic Science Learning Center at the University of Utah. (n.d.). Insights from identical twins. Retrieved August 20, 2015, from http://learn.genetics.utah.edu/content/epigenetics/twins/

Lewis, T. (2014, August 11). Twins separated at birth reveal staggering influence of genetics. Live Science. Retrieved August 18, 2015, from http://www.livescience.com/47288-twin-study-importance-of-genetics.html

Lykken, D. (1999). *Happiness: What studies on twins show us about nature, nurture, and the happiness set point.* New York: Golden Books.

Prohibit genetically engineered babies [video]. (2013, February 13). Intelligence Squared Debates. Retrieved August 11, 2015, from http://intelligencesquaredus.org/debates/upcoming-debates/item/798-prohibit-genetically-engineered-babies

The University of Queensland. (2015, May 19). Nature v nurture: research shows it's both. Retrieved August 18, 2015, from https://www.uq.edu.au/news/article/2015/05/nature-v-nurture-research-shows-its-both

Chapter One: Setting Kids Up for Success

Asplund, J., Agrawal, S., Hodges, T., Harter, J., & Lopez, S.J. (March 2014). *The Clifton StrengthsFinder 2.0 technical report: Development and validation.* Washington, D.C.: Gallup.

Beane, J. (1982). Self-concept and self-esteem as curriculum issues. *Educational Leadership*, 39(7), 504-506.

Bloom, B.S. (1985). *Developing talent in young people.* New York: Ballantine Books.

Cheng, A. (2012, January 25). The unknown story behind Michelle Obama's fashion designer [blog post]. Retrieved April 28, 2015, from http://www.parentwonder.com/michelle-obamas-fashion-designer/

Clifton, D.O., & Nelson, P. (1992). *Soar with your strengths.* New York: Delacorte Press.

Csikszentmihalyi, M., & Schneider, B. (2001). *Becoming adult: How teenagers prepare for the world of work.* New York: Basic Books.

Goertzel, V., & Goertzel, M.G. (1962). *Cradles of eminence.* New York: Little, Brown and Company.

Heller, K. (2015, February 24). Star talker: Neil deGrasse Tyson on fame, education and tweets. *The Washington Post.* Retrieved April 24, 2015, from http://www.washingtonpost.com/lifestyle/style/star-talker-neil-degrasse-tyson-on-fame-education-and-tweets/2015/02/24/5ec101fa-b854-11e4-a200-c008a01a6692_story.html

Lead with your strengths. (n.d.). Retrieved December 2, 2014, from https://www.gallupstrengthscenter.com/

McKay, J., & Greengrass, M. (2003). People. *Monitor on Psychology*, 34(3), 87.

Menkes, S. (2013, September 6). Jason Wu: The American dream. *The New York Times*. Retrieved April 24, 2015, from http://www.nytimes.com/2013/09/07/fashion/jason-wu-on-his-label-and-Hugo-Boss.html?_r=1%20-%20story-continues-1

Person of the week: Fashion designer Jason Wu's inaugural nod [video]. (2013, January 25). ABC News. Retrieved April 24, 2015, from http://abcnews.go.com/WNT/video/person-week-fashion-designer-jason-wus-inaugural-nod-18319315

Positivity. (n.d.). About the author. Retrieved January 22, 2015, from http://www.positivityratio.com/author.php

Rath, T. (2007). *StrengthsFinder 2.0.* New York: Gallup Press.

Rath, T., & Clifton, D.O. (2004). *How full is your bucket?: Positive strategies for work and life.* New York: Gallup Press.

Sherr, L. (2014, January 11). Neil deGrasse Tyson: *Cosmo's* master of the universe. *Parade*. Retrieved April 24, 2015, from http://parade.com/249139/lynnsherr/neil-degrasse-tyson-cosmos-master-of-the-universe/

Wilson, E. (2009, January 23). The spotlight finds Jason Wu. *The New York Times*. Retrieved April 28, 2015, from http://www.nytimes.com/2009/01/25/fashion/25WU.html?emc=eta1

Chapter Two: Can Weaknesses Be Fixed?

Asplund, J. (2012, September 27). When Americans use their strengths more, they stress less. Retrieved May 19, 2015, from http://www.gallup.com/poll/157679/americans-strengths-stress-less.aspx

Asplund, J. (2013, December 27). In U.S., using strengths more may be the best pain medicine. Retrieved May 19, 2015, from http://www.gallup.com/poll/166604/using-strengths-may-best-pain-medicine.aspx

Bernstein, F. (1986). *The Jewish mothers' hall of fame.* Garden City, NY: Doubleday.

Bernstein, F. (1990, December). The world is going to hear of this boy. Retrieved December 15, 2014, from http://www.fredbernstein.com/articles/display.asp?id=45

Bloom, B.S. (1985). *Developing talent in young people.* New York: Ballantine Books.

Buckingham, M. (2001, March 16). Focus on your strengths or fix your weaknesses? Retrieved January 22, 2015, from http://www.gallup.com/poll/1894/focus-your-strengths-fix-your-weaknesses.aspx

Clifton, D.O., & Nelson, P. (1992). *Soar with your strengths.* New York: Delacorte Press.

Daskal, L. (2014, October 9). 100 motivational quotes that will inspire you to succeed. Retrieved June 4, 2015, from http://www.inc.com/lolly-daskal/100-motivational-quotes-that-will-inspire-you-to-succeed.html

Dudley-Marling, C. (2007). Return of the deficit. *Journal of Educational Controversy, 2*(1). Retrieved September 9, 2015, from http://cedar.wwu.edu/cgi/viewcontent.cgi?article=1028&context=jec

Grover, R. (1998, July 13). Steven Spielberg: The storyteller. Retrieved December 15, 2014, from http://www.businessweek.com/1998/28/b3586001.htm

Gupta, P. (2012, October 20). Five things you probably didn't know about Steven Spielberg. Retrieved December 15, 2014, from http://www.salon.com/2012/10/22/five_things_you_probably_didnt_know_about_stephen_spielberg/

Petrosino, A., Turpin-Petrosino, C., & Buehler, J. (2004, April 4). "Scared straight" and other juvenile awareness programs for preventing juvenile delinquency. Retrieved April 24, 2015, from http://www.campbellcollaboration.org/

Rath, T. (2007). *StrengthsFinder 2.0.* New York: Gallup Press.

Rodriguez, C. (2014, June 26). Watch: Steven Spielberg talks dyslexia, "The Goonies" & how the movies saved him. Retrieved December 5, 2014, from http://blogs.indiewire.com/theplaylist/watch-steven-spielberg-talks-dyslexia-the-goonies-how-the-movies-saved-him-20140626

Spence, R. (2013, November 22). The purpose of life and playing to your strengths. Retrieved May 15, 2015, from http://coaching.gallup.com/2013/11/the-purpose-of-life-and-playing-to-your.html

Streeter, R., & Peterson, R. (2012, October 21). Spielberg: A director's life reflected in film. *60 Minutes.* [Television broadcast]. New York: CBS News.

Chapter Three: There's No "Right" Way to Parent

All Nobel Peace Prizes. (n.d.). Retrieved July 1, 2015, from http://www. nobelprize.org/nobel_prizes/peace/laureates/

Angley, N. (2011, September 6). Changing the world through art. CNN. Retrieved January 28, 2015, from http://www.cnn.com/2011/US/08/19/ jeffhanson/

Brazelton, T.B., & Greenspan, S.I. (2000). *The irreducible needs of children: What every child must have to grow, learn, and flourish*. Cambridge, MA: Perseus Publishing.

Brendtro, L.K., Brokenleg, M., & Van Bockern, S. (2009). *Reclaiming youth at risk: Our hope for the future* (Rev. ed.). Bloomington, IN: Solution Tree.

Friedman, L. (2013, July 22). Legally blind artist raises $1 million with his art. *USA Today*. Retrieved January 28, 2015, from http://www.usatoday.com/ story/news/nation/2013/07/21/legally-blind-artist-painting/2499559/

Grandin, T. (2002, January 1). Animals are not things. Retrieved December 9, 2014, from http://www.grandin.com/welfare/animals.are.not.things.html

Grandin, T. (2009). How does visual thinking work in the mind of a person with autism? A personal account. *Philosophical Transactions of the Royal Society B: Biological Sciences, 364*(1522), 1437-1442.

Grandin, T., & Johnson, C. (2006). *Animals in translation: Using the mysteries of autism to decode animal behavior*. Boston: Harcourt, Inc.

Hanson, H. (2013). *Lessons from CLOD: An inspiring story of art, philanthropy and entrepreneurship*. United States: Harold Hanson.

Reckmeyer, M., deBrown, K., & Muller, G.D. (1985). *Significant adult parenting processes.* Lincoln, NE: SRI Perceiver Academies, Inc.

Stumbling blocks for the autistic — often conceptions rather than ability. (n.d.). Retrieved December 9, 2014, from http://www.templegrandin. com/

Temple Grandin biography. (n.d.). Retrieved April 27, 2015, from http:// www.biography.com/people/temple-grandin-38062

Watson, J., & Watson, R. (1928). *Psychological care of infant and child.* New York: W.W. Norton & Company.

Withey, L. (2002). *Dearest friend: A life of Abigail Adams.* New York, NY: Touchstone.

Chapter Four: Your Parenting Strengths

Asplund, J., Agrawal, S., Hodges, T., Harter, J., & Lopez, S.J. (March 2014). *The Clifton StrengthsFinder 2.0 technical report: Development and validation.* Washington, D.C.: Gallup.

University of Melbourne. (2015, May 27). Strength-based parenting improves children's resilience and stress levels. ScienceDaily. Retrieved July 1, 2015, from http://www.sciencedaily.com/releases/2015/05/150527103106.htm

Wagner, R., & Muller, G. (2009). *Power of 2.* New York: Gallup Press.

Chapter Five: Understanding Your Children's Strengths

Butterman, E. (August 2013). A teenager's dream: Algae. ASME.org. Retrieved September 9, 2015, from https://www.asme.org/engineering-topics/articles/renewable-energy/a-teenagers-dream-algae

Caspi, A., Harrington, H., Milne, B., Amell, J.W., Theodore, R.F., & Moffitt, T.E. (2003). Children's behavioral styles at age 3 are linked to their adult personality traits at age 26. *Journal of Personality, 71*, 495-514.

McGraw, C. (2013, March 13). Cheyenne Mountain senior wins $100,000 science award. *The Gazette.* Retrieved September 9, 2015, from http://gazette.com/cheyenne-mountain-senior-wins-100000-science-award/article/152201

McMahon, M. (2015, February 26). Strengths-based parenting. How to build on the positive [blog post]. Retrieved June 10, 2015, from http://upparentingcreek.com/strengths-based-parenting-how-to-build-on-the-positive/

Sara Volz — science is for all ages [TEDxOrangeCoast event]. (2013, November 2). Retrieved September 9, 2015, from http://www.tedxorangecoast.com/videopick/sara-volz-science-ages/

Sara Volz, 17-year-old, makes groundbreaking algae biofuel lab in her bedroom and wins $100,000 scholarship. (2013, March 29). The Huffington Post. Retrieved September 9, 2015, from http://www.huffingtonpost.com/2013/03/29/sara-volz-17-year-old-mak_n_2979408.html

TEDxOrangeCoast 2013 speakers. Sara Volz. Retrieved September 9, 2015, from http://www.tedxorangecoast.com/speakercat/2013/

Chapter Six: Strengths-Based Schools

Bronson, P., & Merryman, A. (2009). *NurtureShock: New thinking about children.* New York: Twelve.

Busteed, B. (2014, September 25). The blown opportunity. *Inside Higher Ed.* Retrieved February 4, 2015, from https://www.insidehighered.com/views/2014/09/25/essay-about-importance-mentors-college-students

Calderon, V. (2014, April 14). How to spot and develop extreme teaching talent. Retrieved February 10, 2015, from http://www.gallup.com/opinion/gallup/173618/spot-develop-extreme-teaching-talent.aspx

Chetty, R., Friedman, J.N., & Rockoff, J.E. (2014, March 1). The long-term impacts of teachers: Teacher value-added and student outcomes in adulthood. Retrieved February 4, 2015, from http://obs.rc.fas.harvard.edu/chetty/value_added.html

Clifton, D.O., & Nelson, P. (1992). *Soar with your strengths.* New York: Delacorte Press.

Gallup. (2014). *State of America's schools: The path to winning again in education.* Washington, D.C.: Gallup.

Gallup & Education Week. (2014, July 1). *Understanding perspectives on American public education: Results of a Gallup-Education Week survey of K-12 school district superintendents.* Washington, D.C.: Gallup.

Gallup, Purdue University, Lumina Foundation, & Healthways. (2014). *Great job, great lives: The 2014 Gallup-Purdue Index Report.* Washington, D.C.: Gallup.

Gordon, G. (2013, July). *School leadership linked to engagement and student achievement.* Washington, D.C.: Gallup.

Highlights of the 2012 PDK/Gallup poll: What Americans said about the public schools [Electronic version]. (2012). *Phi Delta Kappan, 94*, 8-25.

Levine, M. (2005). *Ready or not, here life comes.* New York: Simon & Schuster.

Lopez, S.J., & Louis, M.C. (2009). The principles of strengths-based education [Electronic version]. *Journal of College and Character, 10*(4).

Reavis, G. (n.d.). The animal school: A fable. Retrieved April 24, 2015, from http://agsc.tamu.edu/384/AnimalSchool.pdf

Chapter Seven: Belief, Support, Appreciation

Hammond, W. (2014). Preparing our children to thrive: A strengths-based approach to parenting. Retrieved June 9, 2015, from http://www.esd.ca/Programs/Resiliency/Documents/Preparing%20our%20children%20to%20Thrive.pdf

Clifton StrengthsFinder

Discover your strengths. (n.d.). Retrieved June 4, 2015, from http://www.gallup.com/products/170957/clifton-strengthsfinder.aspx

Gallup created the science of strengths (n.d.). Retrieved June 4, 2015, from https://www.gallupstrengthscenter.com/Home/en-US/About

Clifton Youth StrengthsExplorer

Asplund, J.W., Harter, J.K., & Lopez, S.J. (2015). *Clifton Youth StrengthsExplorer technical report: Development and initial validation.* Washington, D.C.: Gallup.

StrengthsSpotting

Caspi, A., Harrington, H., Milne, B., Amell, J.W., Theodore, R.F., & Moffitt, T.E. (2003). Children's behavioral styles at age 3 are linked to their adult personality traits at age 26. *Journal of Personality, 71,* 495-514.

Acknowledgements

Many years ago, my father and I began formulating the idea of parenting based on strengths. We wanted to capture the concept of talent development as we watched it unfold in so many ways across time and place, showcased at its best, focusing on what is right about people. It has been a work in progress, a work shaped by our understanding of human development, of identifying strengths in adults and children. As clients, coaches and people from all walks of life experienced StrengthsFinder, they have continued to ask how StrengthsFinder can be integrated into that which is nearest to their hearts — their families. To that, our response is *Strengths Based Parenting*. And to that end, I thank the endless knowledge and work of my dad, Don Clifton, whose research and ideas continue today. Of course, without his lifelong partner, my mom Shirley, who has been the glue and "family gatherer" over the decades, this wouldn't have been possible.

Since this is a book about parents and children, I am pleased to begin by thanking my family. They have each played an important role personally and/or professionally. From giving advice, direction, support or just plain real-life experience, both my immediate and extended family who may or may not have known, I was always listening, collecting and watching. To my children, Mike, Andy, Lauren and Mark; my husband, Matt Reckmeyer; and my siblings, Connie Rath, Jim Clifton and Jane Miller.

To the writing and editing partners who added, deleted and shared their expertise: Geoff Brewer, Kelly Henry and Jennifer Robison, along with the rest of their team who helped create and design this book, Samantha Allemang, Trista Kunce and Chin-Yee Lai.

To the many Gallup associates who have added thought, research, content, quotes, action items and examples: Curt Liesveld, Jim Harter, Jim Asplund, JerLene Mosley, Brandon Busteed, Tom Rath, Tom Matson, Rosanne Liesveld, Nancy Oberst, Gale Muller, Tim Hodges, Diann Kroos, Mandy Shelsta, Heather Wright, Scott Wright, Shane Lopez, Jon Clifton, Seth Schuchman, Ed Miller, Gwen Elliott, Valerie Calderon, Jennifer Gardner, Jim Krieger, Phil Ruhlman, Mark Pogue, Paul Allen, Kristin Gregory, Johnathan Tozer, Emily Meyer, Gina Higgins, Leigh Gobber and all the Child Development Center teachers.

Thank you to the strengths coaches from around the world who have shared their experiences; to the parents, kids, educators; to people sitting next to me — on airplanes over the past four decades who had no clue why I asked them so many questions about their childhood, on bleachers and in focus groups who have given me glimpses of excellence in development.

This book truly does exist as a result of countless people — people whose work, insights and research have made major contributions to developing the talents of young and old alike from all walks of life. It takes a village to raise a child, and it takes a village to create a book about parents and children. In gratitude of the village who shared their wisdom, experiences, research and longitudinal perspective.

About the Author

Mary Reckmeyer, Ph.D., is the Executive Director of Gallup's Donald O. Clifton Child Development Center in Omaha, Nebraska. Under her leadership, the center has received national attention for excellence in early childhood education, workplace contribution and developmental results and has helped thousands of children build their lives around their strengths. The center has served as a model for schools nationwide and as a training center for teacher development and education.

Reckmeyer has been with Gallup for more than 30 years. She has served as an Educational and Strengths-Based Development Consultant and Seminar Leader; studied talent-based interviews of more than 2,000 individuals, including children, teachers and parents; and helped create the Clifton Youth StrengthsExplorer, an assessment designed to identify talent in young people. Reckmeyer also coauthored *How Full Is Your Bucket? For Kids*, based on the #1 *New York Times* bestseller *How Full Is Your Bucket?*

Reckmeyer is a former teacher who holds degrees in education and educational psychology. Her research has included youth strengths development, parents of minority achieving students, learning disabilities, educational programming and lifespan development. She has studied outstanding schools and has conducted formal research into what makes an outstanding child care center.

Reckmeyer and her husband live in Lincoln, Nebraska, and have four children.

Gallup Press exists to educate and inform the people who govern, manage, teach and lead the world's 7 billion citizens. Each book meets Gallup's requirements of integrity, trust and independence and is based on Gallup-approved science and research.